99 ways
to raise
SPIRITUALLY
HEALTHY
CHILDREN

99

SPIRITUALLY

KATHLEEN LONG BOSTROM

ways to raise
HEALTHY CHILDREN

WESTMINSTER
JOHN KNOX PRESS
LOUISVILLE · KENTUCKY

1st edition
Published by Westminster John Knox Press
Louisville, Kentucky

10 11 12 13 14 15 16 17 18 19—10 9 8 7 6 5 4 3 2 1

Book design by Drew Stevens
Cover design by designpointinc.com
Cover illustration: © iStockphoto.com

Library of Congress Cataloging-in-Publication Data

Bostrom, Kathleen Long.
   99 ways to raise spiritually healthy children / Kathleen Long Bostrom.
     p. cm.
   Includes bibliographical references (p.   ) and index.
   ISBN 978-0-664-23536-9 (alk. paper)
   1. Parents—Religious life. 2. Parenting—Religious aspects—Christianity.
3. Child rearing—Religious aspects--Christianity. I. Title.
   BV4529.B673 2010
   248.8'45--dc22

2010027046

PRINTED IN THE UNITED STATES OF AMERICA

♾ The paper used in this publication meets the minimum requirements of the American National Standard for Information Sciences—Permanence of Paper for Printed Library Materials, ANSI Z39.48-1992

In loving memory of my father,
Myron C. "Mike" Long
May 17, 1926–August 16, 2010
Dad, you were always the image of God to me.
I will love you forever.

To my three amazing children,
Christopher, Amy, David.
You are my greatest joy,
and I love you more than words can say.

Introduction

At last—here it is, in one manageable book: everything you need to know to raise spiritually healthy children. Simply plow through the list of ninety-nine, check them off as you go, and voilà! You are assured children who will overflow with spiritual health for the rest of their lives.

If only this were possible! Alas, no one resource can sum up everything we need to know as parents. This book is by no means the definitive guide. It provides ideas that I hope will be helpful as you undertake this most worthy of responsibilities: raising a child in a home where spiritual health is not only valued but also lived out day after day.

What is your definition of a spiritually healthy child? One who never misses a Sunday at church? One who agrees with everything you believe? One who can rattle off Bible verses without blinking an eye? If these are your only definitions of a spiritually healthy child, this book may not be for you. Or maybe it's exactly the book you need.

"Spirituality is the pattern by which we shape our lives in response to our experience of God as a very real presence in and around us," Howard Rice writes.[1] Even the tasks that may seem unrelated to faith, such as portioning out the daily chores or deciding how we handle our finances, are reflections of our faith in a living, loving, and forgiving God. God does not expect us to be perfect. God abounds in grace, and we rely on that grace over and over again as we raise our children.

The ideas and activities presented in this book do not appear in hierarchical order, with 1 the most important and 99 the least (although if you read only two, read 1 and 99). Flip through the book and see what catches your eye. You will find a variety of suggestions: activities that families can do together, approaches to participating in church, thoughts on connecting kids to God, and encouragements for parents to care for their own self and soul. Will anyone want to take on all ninety-nine? Probably not, although you're welcome to try. My hope is that in these pages you will find a few insights, a couple of new strategies, several ideas you want to try, and, in the midst of it all, a sense of the grace of God at work in your children and in you.

Each entry includes a Bible verse to serve as a foundation and ends with a thought-provoking question that you can use as a springboard to further thought. The question can be one you share with your family or keep to yourself. It can be used as a journaling prompt if you are so inclined.

The ninety-nine ideas laid out in this book are hardly my own, and you may have a few you could add. I have gleaned from experts: Christian educators, child psychologists, other parents, and children. I have drawn on my own experience as a parent and as a pastor, but I am no authority. My husband and I have raised three amazing children, and they are living proof that parents can make plenty of mistakes and still end up with terrific kids. While ministry has been my active vocation throughout my children's lives, mostly I consider myself to be just one of many mothers who love their children beyond imagining and hope they will live holy and joyful lives.

Bless you as you nurture your child's faith, and your own as well.

Kathleen Long Bostrom
Fall 2010

Contents

Use the space below to keep track of the 99 things as you and your family work on them. Perhaps your kids would like to fill in their own stars!

47	Get to know people of all ages	
48	Practice hospitality	
49	Share chores	
50	Discuss what you've learned at church	
51	Express physical affection	
52	Choose a family song	
53	Tackle the tough topics	
54	Read aloud	
55	Have a secret signal	
56	Create a safe retreat	
57	Turn off the TV	
58	Cook meals together	
59	Be still	
60	Ask the right questions	
61	Be honest	
62	Fill in your family faith tree	
63	Read the Bible together	
64	Say thank you	
65	Get to know your child's friends	
66	Set boundaries	
67	Celebrate for no reason	
68	Make manners matter	
69	Explore the sacraments	
70	Be the parent	
71	Write letters to your child	
72	Be a peacemaker	
73	Teach healthy sexuality	
74	Learn to say no	
75	Fill your home with music	

1 *Be a pretty good parent*

You don't have to be a perfect parent. There's no such thing, in fact.

We enter parenthood with the very best intentions. We read every parenting book we can get our hands on, have thoughtful discussions with other parents, take childbirth classes, paint and decorate the nursery, pick out the safest car seat and stroller, stock up on clothes and diapers and all kinds of paraphernalia. We dream about the ways we will love our child as no child has ever been loved. We promise that we won't make the same mistakes our parents made. We will be consistently loving, patient, gentle, supportive, wise; the perfect parent.

And then reality hits. This parenting stuff is hard work! Endless work. Rewarding but impossible work. We may continue to have all of our good intentions, but it's easy to get discouraged with all the ways we fall short of our own expectations.

You are going to make mistakes. Notice the plural use of that word. You are going to make more than one mistake, and you'll even make the same mistake more than once. You will make big mistakes and small mistakes and mistakes of all sizes in-between. You are going to lose your temper and your patience. You are going to say and do things you wish you hadn't, and not do and say things you wish you had. You can dwell on the mistakes, or you can learn from them and move on.

You don't have to be a perfect parent. Strive to be a "pretty good parent," a "good enough parent," as some describe it.[2] Pretty good is good enough.

Three words can be helpful: remind, recognize, and remember.

REMIND yourself that you are only human. Let yourself off the hook. Forgive yourself for what you perceive as failure. When your best intentions fall flat, shrug it off. Don't get bogged down by making lists in your head of all the ways you failed your child. Move forward, not backward. Laugh at yourself.

RECOGNIZE that many factors are out of your control. You can't plan when you or your child will get sick, or when your car will break down, or when the punk at the playground will say something mean that ruins your child's day. The best-laid plans fly out the window along with the odor of the burnt casserole that was supposed to be a wonderful family dinner. Life happens. Go with the flow. Save your sweat for the big stuff.

REMEMBER the big picture and believe that your child is going to be fine, despite your best and worst efforts. Overall, the sum of the good you've done will be greater than all the bits and pieces you wish you could change. Remember that you are not in this alone. Put your parenting skills in God's hands. Pray about your decisions. Trust God to bring good out of even the toughest of times. Believe in grace.

Say to yourself, even when you hardly believe it, "I am a good mother." "I am a good father." Trust yourself to be a pretty good parent, good enough, not a perfect parent. You are the perfect parent for your child.

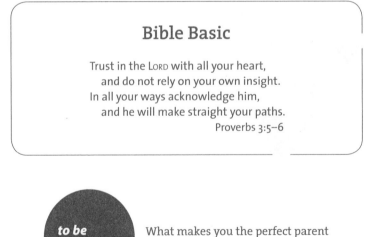

Bible Basic

Trust in the Lord with all your heart,
   and do not rely on your own insight.
In all your ways acknowledge him,
   and he will make straight your paths.
Proverbs 3:5–6

to be continued . . .   What makes you the perfect parent for your particular child?

2 *Allow room for doubt*

We tiptoe around doubts, afraid that if we express them, we are exhibiting a lack of faith. We have doubts about everything else in the world, from relationships to the brand of toothpaste we always thought was best, but we are often reluctant to express doubts when it comes to faith. We seem to think that if we have doubts about God, then we're doing something wrong, or our faith isn't very strong.

Doubts help us figure things out. If we are in a relationship we thought was going to result in marriage, but then start having doubts, we need to ask ourselves a few questions. "Are my doubts an indication that this is not a healthy relationship; or are they simply a result of my own cold feet because, after going through a nasty divorce, I have a hard time trusting that someone truly loves me?"

Doubt is an acceptable part of faith, and it is expressed over and over again in the Bible. The Psalms are full of questions and doubts expressed by people of faith. "Why, O LORD, do you stand far off? Why do you hide yourself in times of trouble?" (Psalm 10:1). Doubts arise out of anguish and pain, but also out of a healthy curiosity and a seeking of truth.

In the New Testament, the apostle Thomas gets a bad rap. After the resurrection, when Jesus first appeared to the disciples, Thomas wasn't in the room. When he heard that Jesus had returned, he wanted to see for himself. The poor guy has been dubbed Doubting Thomas ever since, even though he had been, and continued to be, a faithful follower of Jesus. His doubts didn't make him less of a disciple than the other ten.

Doubts can be aimed at the very existence of God: "Is God just a figment of our imaginations?" Doubts can also be a way of figuring out how God works (or doesn't work): "I don't think God really cares about people or there wouldn't be so many terrible things that happen." In either case, doubts are a way of wrestling with the doctrines we've been taught, so that we can come to a firm understanding of what we believe based on our own experience of God.

Clergyman and author Frederick Buechner writes, "Doubt is the ants in the pants of faith. It keeps it alive and kicking."[3] Think of doubts as part of the ongoing faith conversation. Doubts can help us clarify what we already believe or lead us into a deeper understanding of issues we never had thought about before. The psalms that start off questioning God and God's care for the people end up as affirmations of faith: "But you do see! Indeed you note trouble and grief, that you may take it into your hands" (Psalm 10:14). Doubts make us think deeply about what we truly believe. Our most troubling doubts may lead to our greatest affirmations of faith.

Bible Basic

I believe; help my unbelief!
Mark 9:24

to be continued...

What doubt has helped to keep your faith "alive and kicking"?

3 *Be kind*

The poet William Wordsworth wrote, "On that best portion of a good man's life; / His little, nameless, unremembered acts / Of kindness and of love."[4] If you are a person who practices kindness, you can be sure that your kindness will bless the lives of others, even if you never know exactly how someone's life was changed because of you.

Kindness is not a lost art, although it may seem that way when your child is being tormented by a bully at school or when your boss treats you as if your opinions don't matter.

There's more than enough rudeness to go around, but it can be diffused and diminished when kindness is practiced.

Some years ago, noticing and performing "random acts of kindness" became a trend. Books were published about it, and people were encouraged to do random acts as a way of making society kinder. The trend may not be as visible these days, but it's not defunct. The Random Acts of Kindness Foundation was incorporated in 1995 as a 501(c)(3) nonprofit organization, dedicated to promoting acts of kindness. Its Web site (www. actsofkindness.org) offers detailed ways to promote and participate in acts of kindness at home, in the classroom, in the community, and throughout the world. The site also explains how being kind is good for your health. Maybe kindness is a fitness plan we can all adopt!

The Golden Rule states that we should treat other people as we wish to be treated ourselves and that we should *not* treat people as we would *not* like to be treated. There are subtle differences here. We treat other people as we wish to be treated: with kindness, respect, compassion, and love. We can also choose not to engage in behavior that is rude, cruel, and unkind.

The Golden Rule is found in many cultures and faith traditions. When Jesus gave his first sermon to thousands of eager listeners, he included the Golden Rule. It wasn't a new idea, but his use of it reemphasized the importance of this rule and made it a requirement for all who choose to follow in Jesus' footsteps.

The Golden Rule is golden for a good reason. Treating others as you want to be treated is a priceless gift, and if everyone practiced kindness on a regular basis, this world would be a lot closer to being the peaceable kingdom that God desires.

"Kindness gives birth to kindness," wrote the philosopher Sophocles.[5] Kindness is the gift that keeps on giving.

Bible Basic

As God's chosen ones, holy and beloved, clothe yourselves with compassion, kindness, humility, meekness, and patience.

Colossians 3:12

"In everything do to others as you would have them do to you."

Matthew 7:12

to be continued ...

Have you been the recipient of a random act of kindness? Share this with your children.

4 *Prepare for worship*

More and more churches are child friendly these days. A congregation that welcomes children in worship expects a little noise and commotion. But children should be prepared for what they will experience in a worship service, not only for reasons of etiquette, but because worship will be a lot more meaningful if children understand what's going on.

Whether you have kept your child with you in worship from the time that child was born or are introducing your child to a church service for the first time, there are steps you can take to engage your child in worship. An effective way to begin teaching your child about worship is to go to church sometime other than a Sunday morning.

Call the church office and find out what time the church building is open during the week. Ask to speak with a pastor or Christian education director, and arrange to bring your child to church to do some exploring.

At the church, introduce your child to the person who is guiding you on your "tour." Children need to learn how to interact with adults, and this is a good place to begin.

Get to know the layout of the church facility. Find out the locations of child care, church school classes, bathrooms. You and your child will be more comfortable in worship if you also know your way around the rest of the building.

Take your child into the sanctuary. Let the child see how it feels to sit in a pew or on a chair. If there are hymnbooks or Bibles, let the child leaf through the pages, and explain how the books are used. Take the child to the front of the church, and let the child peek behind the pulpit or Communion table.

Pick up a worship bulletin and go over the service at home. Explain that there are times to stand and times to sit, times to sing or pray or listen. If the Lord's Prayer is included, go over the words ahead of time. Prepare an offering, using envelopes from the church or one from home, and let your child put the money in the envelope.

Play "let's go to church" at home, using the different components of the worship service. This may be more effective than trying to overload your child with too much information at once.

The best way for your children to be comfortable in worship is to bring them to worship on a regular basis. It may try your patience on occasion, but sooner or later, they'll get the hang of it, and it will be well worth the effort.

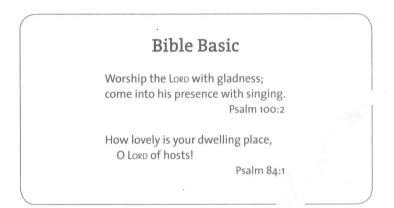

Bible Basic

Worship the LORD with gladness;
come into his presence with singing.

Psalm 100:2

How lovely is your dwelling place,
O LORD of hosts!

Psalm 84:1

to be continued . . .

What do you remember about the first time you attended a service of worship?

5 *Follow through*

We've seen the scene a thousand times. Often, we play the parts.

Parent and child are in the grocery store. The child is grabbing items from the shelves, whining, "I want this! I want this!"

The parent, obviously exasperated, raises her voice. "You put that back on the shelf right now, or I'm not buying you anything!"

Repeat. Several times.

Finally worn down, embarrassed at being observed by strangers, or simply tired of her child's whining, the parent gives in. Even her voice changes to a syrupy tone. "OK, honey, just that one bag of cookies, then."

It appears that the child wins, but both parent and child are the losers in this game.

The child learns very quickly that "If I just push and push and keep asking, Mom will give me what I want." There are no consequences to the child's unacceptable behavior. The real lesson learned by the child is that "Mom never follows through; her words are meaningless."

If you say you're going to do something, do it. Children need to know that there are consequences to their behavior, good or bad.

When the parent is consistent about following through with promises (and threats), the child learns to trust the parent. There is a sense of security for the child, knowing that Mom or Dad say what they mean and mean what they say. Consistency and follow-through put some secure and much-needed boundaries around the child. When parents follow through, they're not only lessening the chance that the child will beg for treats at the store every time they go shopping, they're also increasing the chance that their children will know that when they get out of control, the parents will be there to get them back on track.

Don't make a statement so exaggerated that you can't follow through with it. "If you don't stop whining, you're not going to play outside for a month!" Is that manageable? Do you *want* to have an unhappy child sitting indoors for four weeks? It's an empty threat, and children know it. They're very smart! And persistent. "If you don't stop whining now, you will not watch your favorite TV show tonight" is a warning with which you can actually follow through.

Follow through when you promise something positive, too. "If you clean up your room now, we'll have time to go out for ice cream after dinner." Don't say that if you know you have to rush off to a meeting right after the dishes are done and there is no time to go out for ice cream even if the child does clean his room. Beware of empty promises you can't keep.

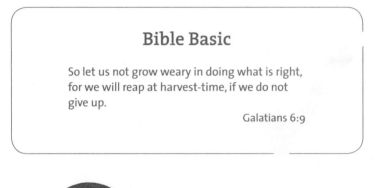

Bible Basic

So let us not grow weary in doing what is right, for we will reap at harvest-time, if we do not give up.

Galatians 6:9

to be continued . . .

How do you feel when someone makes a promise to you that can't be kept?

6 *Keep a gratitude journal*

Whether or not you keep a journal or diary of any other kind, try to keep a gratitude journal.

A gratitude journal is a blank book that you fill with daily expressions of gratitude. Every night, jot down one thing for which you are grateful. No matter how terrible your day has been, find something, even if it is, "I got through the day." You don't have to write a detailed explanation; a line or two will do.

Keep your own personal gratitude journal, and start another one to use as a family. As part of your nighttime ritual, and perhaps as important as making sure the kids brush their teeth, take a moment to reflect on what your family is grateful for each day. Ask your children what they are thankful for. Be ready for a slew of responses, especially from the youngest members of the family!

If this brief time of reflection fits your schedule better at the dinner table, do it then. Find a time when all of you are gathered together, and elicit a group response. On those days when you can't all sit down at the same time (which happens more and more as children get older and busier with outside activities), leave the journal in a place where each child can jot down a few quick words of thanks.

As with any journaling exercise, don't beat yourself up if you don't write in the journal every day. Do the best you can. Don't turn this into a chore (see entry 49). But know that the more you make this a priority, the more you will start finding reasons to give thanks during the course of your day, not just at the end of it.

When you need a lift, go back and read through your list of "gratitudes." You'll see the pattern of a grateful heart that can always find something for which to give thanks.

Bible Basic

I am grateful to God—whom I worship with a clear conscience, as my ancestors did—when I remember you constantly in my prayers night and day.

2 Timothy 1:3

to be continued ...   What are you thankful for today?

7 *Learn how to lose*

What's the first question asked when you say you've been to a sporting event?

"Who won?"

If your team lost, you may not be happy to answer that question.

We are obsessed with winning and losing; we idolize people who are winners.

Two people play the final match of a Grand Slam tennis tournament. They are two of the finest tennis players in the world, yet at the end of the match, one wins and one loses. One goes away on top of the world, and the other, equally talented, is filled with disappointment. The trophy of the winner is so much more grand and glorious than that of the loser. Both should feel like winners, but that is nearly impossible the way the system is set up.

Winning can be a great motivation in sports and other competitions. The desire to win makes us work hard to prepare for an event and to do our best, and it's good to have the desire to do well. But winning isn't everything, and it shouldn't be.

Life isn't always about winning. Losses punctuate the whole of it: loss of a competition, loss of a job, loss of dreams, loss of a way of life, and, ultimately, loss of life. Many people never learn how to lose without feeling defeated.

The fear of losing makes some people reluctant to try in the first place, makes them give up on something before even giving it a go. We avoid situations where we might lose, rather than take a chance. Even in relationships, our fear of losing the other person causes us to hold back, to try to protect ourselves from the sorrow that comes with a deep loss.

As parents, we want our kids to feel good about themselves, to be winners in the great game of life, never to experience the sadness of losing. But learning to lose strengthens us to face our inevitable losses without being destroyed by them.

Encourage your children to try new things without worrying about being the best. Acknowledge their sadness or disappointment when they lose, but tell them you're proud of their efforts. Expect them to be gracious losers, to shake hands with the person who won. There's no reason to make excuses or downplay the winner's efforts.

Don't always purposely lose a game just so they can win every time. You're not doing your child any favors.

Be a good sport. Being a gracious loser makes you the winner in the end.

Bible Basic

For those who want to save their life will lose it, and those who lose their life for my sake will find it.

Matthew 16:25

to be continued . . .

What situation have you avoided because you were afraid to lose?

8 *Teach worship etiquette*

The first rule of church etiquette should be "treat God's house as if it were your own," but considering how some people treat their home, that might not be such a good idea!

Church is where we come to worship God in community. Certain rules should be followed, and none of them are all that hard or restrictive. It is common sense to be aware that you aren't the only one sitting in worship and to act accordingly.

Children mimic your behavior, so that puts the pressure on you to exhibit church etiquette. Be intentional about particulars. "Let's put the Bible and the hymnbook back where we found them, so they're ready for the next person." When you leave, take your bulletin with you rather than leaving it on the pew.

Be on time. Being late to worship can happen to anyone, but try not to make it a habit.

Respect the people around you. Whispering, talking, passing notes, or using your cell phone distract the people sitting near you.

Don't use electronics (cell phones, handheld games) during worship. Unless you are a physician or for some other reason need to be reached immediately (a sick child at home, for example), turn your cell phones off completely (otherwise, set them to vibrate). Leave other electronic devices at home. It may be funny when someone's cell phone starts to ring during a prayer, but it's not *that* funny.

Close your eyes or bow your head when you pray. This not only helps you to pay attention to the prayers, it is a courtesy to others. Prayers are not the time to check out what the person behind you is doing or to grab a quick bite to eat.

Don't chew gum, eat, or drink during worship. There is plenty of time to do this after church. If you have a cold or sore throat and need a lozenge, that might be acceptable—except that you shouldn't be in church if you are sick! Don't leave used gum, candy wrappers, or cups on the pew or the floor.

If someone needs to pass by you in the pew, make room for them graciously, not grudgingly. And if you find someone sitting in the pew you usually occupy, don't make a fuss. Most likely, the person didn't sit in "your" pew to annoy you. Find another place and come to church a bit earlier next time.

Learning to worship in community is an important part of spiritual health, since much of our learning takes place in the community of faith. We are a family, so let's at least act like one that gets along and likes one another.

Bible Basic

I was glad when they said to me,
"Let us go to the house of the Lord!"
Psalm 122:1

to be continued . . .

Do you have a pet peeve regarding some aspect of church etiquette?

9 *Play together*

It is said that the family that prays together stays together, but that is just as true with the family that plays together. Fun and laughter can bring families together and ease tensions better than just about anything else.

Play is how children learn. Play is an important part of their development, as they experiment, use their imaginations, figure things out, and fine-tune their large and small motor skills. Play is work, but that doesn't mean it can't be fun. Work as fun? What a concept!

Children learn when they're playing with their parents, too, and they love it when the important adults in their lives take time to play. Children learn how to interact with adults. They learn that their parents care about their world. They learn that adults can be entertaining. Grandparents shouldn't have all the fun, but sometimes we wait until our kids have kids before we learn that playing with the youngest members of the family trumps a lot of other things we tend to put ahead of that.

Plan some playtime: A game night that includes all the ages in your family. A special outing to the park when it's not just the kids swinging on the swings and sliding down the slides. A craft extravaganza where supplies are piled on the table and everyone gets to use their imaginations to create. Do this on a regular basis; schedule it on the calendar.

Planning an intentional fun time is just part of the equation. Be willing to be interrupted, to set aside your own agenda now and then, because that speaks volumes to your child. Stop, drop, and play when you can, because it won't be possible every time. It's OK for children to know you have things you need to get done, but be spontaneous every now and then even if it's for only a few minutes.

Does your church plan social events during the year when adults and children all gather to have fun? If so, make these events a priority. If not, suggest to your pastor that you're willing to help plan an annual picnic at the park, a weekly "open gym" night, or a quarterly potluck/movie/game night at the church or in homes.

Play brings the generations together. The folks whose kids are grown and gone will relish a chance to play with the young ones, and your children get the joy of being with other adults who aren't exhausted with the work of raising children.

Have a playful spirit. It's contagious!

Bible Basic

So I commend enjoyment, for there is nothing better for people under the sun than to eat, and drink, and enjoy themselves, for this will go with them in their toil through the days of life that God gives them under the sun.

Ecclesiastes 8:15

to be continued...

Did your parents take time to play games with you?

10 *Pray together*

Has work got you down? Frightened by what tomorrow may bring? Not sure what to do or where to turn for help? The answer is at your fingertips: put your hands together and pray.

If prayer was part of your daily life growing up, you are probably comfortable with the idea. If you are wrestling with the concept of prayer, learning to pray with your child can open the door for you. If prayer has never been a part of your life, children will drive you to it, so you might as well get started!

Prayers don't have to be long, wordy, and overly detailed. Prayer is a conversation with God. Tell God what's on your heart. Pour out your concerns. Thank God for your blessings and your challenges. Promise you'll talk again real soon, and then do it.

Prayers at mealtime and before bed seem to get the most attention, but try to intersperse your day with prayer. When you wake your child in the morning (or when she wakes you), greet the day, "Thank you, God, for this new day!" When your child comes to you, sobbing because the neighbor ran off to play with someone else, offer a hug and a prayer, "Dear God, we'll be OK, right? Amen!" You don't have to make a big deal about it, or be overly dramatic; but neither should you dismiss the opportunity to connect with God. Ask your child, "Is it OK with you if I say a prayer that God will help you feel better?" Respect the child if she says no. Prayer should never be forced on anyone.

Compile a list of prayer signals. Every time you hear a siren, stop what you're doing and say a prayer. When the alarm goes off in the morning, say a prayer. When you hear the baby cry in the middle of the night, say a prayer.

If your church includes a list of prayer requests in worship, bring the list home and pray for the people during the week.

In their book *How Do You Spell God? Answers to the Big Questions from Around the World*, Marc Gellman and Thomas Hartman write, "The reason all religions have prayers or chants or meditations is that all human beings need to say four things in their lives. Those four things that all people need to say are: Thanks! Wow! Gimme! and Oops!"[6] Use these for a well-rounded prayer life. They're easy to remember.

Children accept the concept of prayer quicker than adults. They aren't burdened down with trying to figure it all out. Your children can learn to pray from watching you, but you can also learn to pray by watching your children.

Praying with your child is a powerful experience. If you want to be truly humbled, ask your child to pray for you. It's good for your child to know that you trust him that much. And you will be blessed beyond measure.

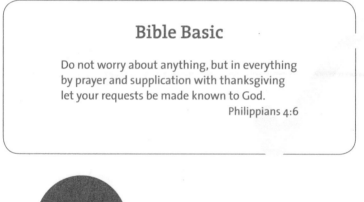

Bible Basic

Do not worry about anything, but in everything by prayer and supplication with thanksgiving let your requests be made known to God.

Philippians 4:6

to be continued . . .

Thanks! Wow! Gimme! Oops! Which prayer do you offer to God today?

11 Practice integrity

Integrity is how you act when nobody is watching.

Integrity is telling the truth, especially when someone is watching.

Integrity is accepting responsibility for your actions, even—and especially—when those actions may not have been right.

Integrity is the backbone of culture, society, family. Without integrity at our core, all our efforts to raise our children to be spiritually healthy people are worthless.

These are strong words, for sure, but strong words are needed when the living of our lives is at stake.

Integrity is best taught when it is modeled by the parent. Children learn to trust when they are raised by people who practice integrity.

If you make a mistake, don't try to hide it. Own up to it. Let your children know that you're not perfect. Let them know that you, and they, can learn from mistakes. What will you do to resolve the problem you've caused? Kids need to see you being responsible for mistakes that you've made.

Be truthful. Too often we hide behind little white lies, thinking they do not matter. They do. When you've planned a family night and a friend calls and invites you out, don't make up an excuse like "I have to work tonight." Tell the truth: "I planned to be home with my family tonight, but I'd love to get together another time."

Do not belittle others. It's OK to disagree with someone or to have an opinion. Cutting people down, calling names, chewing out the waitress in front of your kids because your steak wasn't cooked right is unnecessary, and embarrassing, to your kids more than to anyone else. People who practice integrity will find an honorable way to express themselves that isn't at the cost of another person's dignity.

Respect your child's privacy. Don't go through their personal belongings, read their mail, or eavesdrop. Would you want someone doing this to you? Behave as you wish to be treated. If you respect your children, they are more likely to respect you.

Integrity is the *integration* of what we believe, who we are, and what we do.

When we practice integrity, we live by example, a good example. Your child needs positive role models, and you are the most important role model in the world.

Bible Basic

The righteous walk in integrity
—happy are the children who follow them!

Proverbs 20:7

What public figure do you most admire because of his or her integrity?

12 *Stick together*

In a world where there is so much antagonistic competition, being part of a family that sticks together through thick and thin is a great gift. It's a relief to know there will always be a few people on your side, and vice versa. Your family is a team that works best when every member respects and honors the others.

Your child's friends should not be allowed to tease or antagonize siblings, no matter how irritating they are. Make sure each child has some space when friends are visiting. If little brother is invited to be part of their playtime, fine, but siblings also need space from one another. Still, it is never acceptable for a child's friends to be cruel to other children in the family.

Parents who convey a united front to their children are less likely to see a child try to play one parent against the other. As kids realize that they're not going to get what they want by pitting parents against each other, they'll give up trying to do that.

Avoid using the old "Wait until your father gets home!" ploy. A better response is, "When your father gets home, he and I will figure out what to do about the way you behaved at school today." Parents who do not live in the same home should not criticize the other parent to the children out of their own anger or as an attempt to win the child's favor. Children who alternate time between parents feel divided enough over the situation without parents trying to widen the divide. Take the high road, and if you have a complaint with the other parent, address that directly, not through the child.

In the New Testament, the apostle Paul uses the image of the body to explain how Christians are to build community together. No part is more important than the rest. Every part of the body has something to offer the whole. The body functions in a healthy way when every member is cherished, honored, and encouraged to be unique and yet part of a larger whole, all united by the Spirit of Christ.

Do not overemphasize the "family first" ideal. There is no need to do everything together as a family every moment, every day. You can respect, honor, and love one another even when you're not in the same place. Sometimes, you need a little distance.

"Family first" is a great motto, but it is different from "family only."

Bible Basic

For just as the body is one and has many members, and all the members of the body, though many, are one body, so it is with Christ.

1 Corinthians 12:12

to be continued...

What words would you use to describe your family? Think of three, and then share those with your family.

13 *Bless your child*

A standard response when someone sneezes is to say, "Bless you!" which is shortened from "God bless you." Explanations for how this custom started cannot be verified: People used to think that the soul left the body when a person sneezed, so offering a quick blessing protected the person from evil. The fear that the heart stops during a sneeze might also have prompted the blessing. The custom might have begun in 590 CE during an outbreak of bubonic plague, because sneezing was thought to indicate the onset of the plague. The blessing was a response to the pope's edict that people be in constant prayer to combat the disease.

We may not be sure where the phrase "God bless you" originated, but what does it matter? The fact is, it is a lovely phrase, and even more, it can be part of a holy moment between you and another person. Let that person be your child.

Rachel Naomi Remen is a physician specializing in cancer. She is also the author of the book *My Grandfather's Blessings: Stories of Strength, Refuge, and Belonging*. In this book, Remen recalls that during her childhood she and her grandfather had tea together on Friday afternoons. After they had finished their tea, her grandfather would call the little girl over to stand in front of him. He would gently place his hands on top of her head and thank God for her. "He would specifically mention my struggles during that week and tell God something about me that was true," she writes. "Then he would give me his blessing and ask the long-ago women I knew from his many stories—Sarah, Rachel, Rebekah, and Leah—to watch over me. These few moments were the only time in my week when I felt completely safe and at rest."[7]

We offer our children a blessing when we give thanks to God for their lives and ask for guidance and grace. But how often do we actually place our hands upon our child's head when we pray? Imagine the power and peace of such a moment between parent and child.

Bless your child. Place your hands upon that precious child's head and offer a prayer of thanksgiving. Tell God why you are thankful for that particular child and what you see is special about your child. Babies, toddlers, school-age, teens, young adults: age is not a boundary. If you start early, your child will grow up feeling blessed, and it won't feel strange. Even if your child is a teen and thinks you're losing your mind, place your hands on that child's head and give a blessing.

Bless your child in the middle of the night when she's asleep or when she is sick. Bless your child from a distance, when he is away at summer camp, by placing your hand on his photo.

God bless you. God bless you for loving your child and wanting to be the best parent you can be. God bless you in the journey. God bless you, and your child, too.

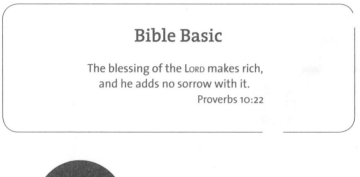

Bible Basic

The blessing of the Lord makes rich,
and he adds no sorrow with it.
Proverbs 10:22

to be continued . . .

What does the phrase "God bless you" mean to you?

14 Volunteer as a family

Families are so busy these days! Even with the modern conveniences that are supposed to make life easier, we seem to have fewer and fewer hours in the day. Family time is at a premium. Many parents and children are stressed out by long work hours and the activities that fill our days to the brim. We long for more, relaxed family time, but it never seems to happen.

Finances are being strained by the cost of living and the downturn of the economy. This adds even more pressure on families.

There are no easy answers to time and economic restraints, but there is something that can reduce the stress from both problems: volunteer as a family.

When we volunteer together, we build ties that bind us not only to each other, but also to the foundations of our faith. Service and outreach to others connects the Bible stories with our own stories. We read about Jesus feeding the hungry, healing the sick, engaging with people who were the outcasts of society. Jesus didn't turn a blind eye to those in need. Indeed, we are even told in the Gospel of Matthew that when we serve others, we serve Christ.

Find out what charities or volunteer organizations are accessible in your area. If you belong to a church (and you should; see entry 22), that's a great place to start. Make a list of what's available, then decide together where you will give your time and efforts. While a worthy organization such as Habitat for Humanity may sound like something you want to do, it may have age limits. Research the details before you sign up.

Many volunteer opportunities can involve family members of various ages. Your church may already be sponsoring a walk to raise money for the hungry. Everyone in the family can participate in this. Strap on baby carriers and borrow a wheelchair. Enlist others to cheer as you walk by. A homeless shelter may need volunteers to lay out sleeping mats, set tables, pack lunches. Young children can design and color place mats to use for the evening meal or make note cards with encouraging messages to put in the lunch bags. All ages can pray for the people who will be sheltered for the night but who face multiple challenges with each new day.

Children learn self-worth when they can help others. They are connected to a larger world, a world that Jesus asked us to care for. Volunteering puts our own lives in perspective. We are moved to give thanks for the basics that we have: a safe place to sleep, food in the refrigerator, a family who loves us, a God who trusts us to look out for one another.

Bible Basic

"Truly I tell you, just as you did it to one of the least of these who are members of my family, you did it to me."

Matthew 25:40

to be continued . . .

Have you ever received help from strangers? Share this with your family.

15 *Encourage independence*

Children are eager learners. You may get tired of hearing "I want to do it myself!" but listen to this plea. Let your child do things for himself, even when you get frustrated or impatient with the process.

It's tempting to step in and do things our way. But how will a child learn to tie her shoes if we insist on tying them every time she puts her shoes on? How will our teenager learn to balance his life if we continually take charge of every detail and never trust him to learn from his mistakes as well as his accomplishments?

You may not intend to convey the message "I don't trust you to figure things out for yourself," but that could be what your child hears when you consistently take charge.

It's not a good idea to let your two-year-old choose his own bedtime every night. You can, however, let him choose what color socks he wears. Small attempts at independence develop confidence and responsibility, which leads to the ability to make wise choices as the choices themselves get more complex.

Our instinct is to protect our children. We mean well when we step in to save the day, but step back a moment and think about the results of being overprotective.

Kids need to learn to face the consequences of their actions. The mother of a second-grader reminds her daughter several times to put her library book by the door before she goes to bed so she won't forget to take it to school in the morning. After her daughter catches the bus the next day, mom sees the book on the floor of her daughter's bedroom. She knows her daughter will lose recess time if she doesn't have the book. Does mom hop in the car and rush the book to school to spare her daughter the consequences of her actions? Not if she wants her daughter to learn to look out for herself.

Think of it as yet another of life's many teachable moments.

As your children grow and become more involved with people and activities outside the home, it is essential that they develop the ability to think on their own and to be confident in their ability to take care of themselves. There are so many choices to make. Parents can provide the tools and the atmosphere that enhance a child's confidence and wise decision making.

Consider yourself to be a consultant rather than a manager. You're there to help your child figure things out, to listen, to offer reflective possibilities, especially as your child gets older. Refuse to get caught up in managing all the details.

When your four-year-old announces, "I tied my own shoes!" you celebrate the joy of her newfound knowledge and accomplishment. When your teenager refuses to get in the car with a friend who is drunk, you'll know that he is well on his way to being an independent and responsible adult.

Believe in your children's abilities so that they can believe in themselves. "You can do it! I believe in you" are words that never get old.

Bible Basic

But we urge you, beloved, . . . to mind your own affairs, . . . so that you may behave properly toward outsiders and be dependent on no one.
1 Thessalonians 4:10–12

to be continued . . .

How do you encourage your child to be independent?

16 *Learn and experience other faith traditions*

With advancements in technology, our view of the world has broadened. With TV, Internet, and the increased speed and accessibility of travel, we are aware that we are not the only folks in the world and that our way of living is not the only way. Even if we live in a homogeneous neighborhood, we are in touch with people who look, act, think, and worship differently than we do.

Learning about other faith traditions and teaching them to your children will not cause them to leave the Christian faith. It will promote tolerance and understanding, open up dialogue, and enrich the practice of your own faith.

Borrow or buy a book that explains the concepts and practices of other faiths. What is the history of each faith? What are the basic theological beliefs? What rituals are a part of their worship? Are there certain foods that are eaten or prohibited? What is the reasoning behind this? Be sensitive to the traditions that seem strange to you.

Find out how other people pray and worship. Do they kneel when they pray, or stand for the entire worship service? Is the Sabbath day celebrated on a day other than Sunday?

Make an effort to celebrate a few non-Christian holidays. Make note of them on your calendar. See if there is a worship service in your area where visitors are welcome. Make a field trip to another house of faith.

If your child has a friend who practices a different faith tradition, you have a wonderful opportunity to learn more about another faith. Attend a bar mitzvah if you are invited. Ask the family over to your home to get to know them and to learn about what they believe and how they worship. This is not a time to try to convert someone to your way of thinking. Keep an open mind, do not judge, ask questions, and celebrate your differences, and your similarities, too.

Incorporate the practices of other faiths into your own spiritual practice. Designate a prayer rug in your living room, where family members can sit or kneel to pray. Light candles at the beginning of the Sabbath meal. Eat less during a season when others are fasting.

Learning about other faith traditions teaches your children tolerance and kindness, and lessens the fear and anger that cause people to lash out at one another in ignorance.

Bible Basic

So then, whenever we have an opportunity, let us work for the good of all, and especially for those of the family of faith.

Galatians 6:10

to be continued...

Have you ever attended worship in a faith home other than your own?

17 *Remember your baptism*

Particular events punctuate our lives, cause us to pause and give thanks for the gift of life. Birthdays are at the top of the list; anniversaries run a close second.

Consider adding baptism to birthdays and anniversaries and the other occasions that are marked with special celebrations.

Baptism is a big deal. When a parent brings a child to the church for baptism, much thought goes into the preparation. Parents meet with the pastor (or should) so that they can understand the meaning of baptism. Particular clothes are chosen for the child to wear. A date is chosen that accommodates family and friends who want to attend.

Baptism marks the entrance of that child (or adult) into the family of faith. God's grace and love are already active in our lives; in baptism, we claim that and promise to cherish the life we have been given, not just on the day of baptism, but forever.

Why not remember our baptism with a party each year? A birthday isn't the only day we should set aside to celebrate the gift of life.

Some churches give a candle to a child on the day of baptism to offer a tangible way to remember the baptism. The candle is taken out and relit every year. Children are told the story of their baptism. The whole family remembers and celebrates the anniversary. Since many people are baptized as infants, they have no concrete memory of their baptism. By celebrating baptism every year, the stories are told and retold and become embedded in the child's memory.

Share with your children the stories of your baptism. What do you remember about that day, if anything? What stories did your family tell you about your baptism? Do you have photos? A baptismal certificate? Who attended your baptism? Did you cry? What did you wear? Some families have a special baptismal gown, passed down through the generations. Did your child wear the same gown you wore when you were baptized? Children love to hear these stories, and it's a fair wager that the adults enjoy them, too.

Celebrate the anniversary of your child's baptism each year, as you do a birthday. Have a special meal, light the baptism candle, offer a prayer. Recall the ways that God has guided and blessed your child's life during the past year, and voice your hopes for the future. Give thanks for the family of faith that has nurtured your child.

"Rather than being momentary events in our lives, the sacraments have meaning for our daily living as God's faithful people."[8]

Bible Basic

There is one body and one Spirit, just as you were called to the one hope of your calling, one Lord, one faith, one baptism, one God and Father of all, who is above all and through all and in all.

Ephesians 4:4–6

to be continued . . .

What is your favorite story about your baptism?

18 *Do more than worship*

Attending a worship service each week is important in raising spiritually healthy children. If you do this, that's great! But you're not off the hook completely. It takes more than a weekly drop-in/drive-away hour to nurture the life of faith.

"The time between church school, worship, and midweek learning opportunities becomes critical in nurturing children in the Christian faith."[9] The way you live in the week between Sundays allows the lessons learned in church to take root, grow, and flourish. The life of faith is not an occasional thing. It is a daily necessity, like eating and sleeping, which you wouldn't dream of doing only once a week.

Need some help? This book expands on many of these suggestions:

Retell the Bible stories you heard in church (entry 63).

Pray, together and by yourself (entry 10).

Sing or listen to music that is worshipful and uplifting (entry 75).

Get involved in a charity or volunteer (entry 14).

Examine current events from your understanding of faith (entry 35).

Celebrate holy days at home (entry 28).

Discuss what you learned in church (entry 50).

There's no need to go to extremes and listen only to Christian music, read only from the Bible, talk only about theology. You want your children to have a well-rounded life, to experience all different kinds of literature, music, and other activities. It's impossible to isolate children from the world, and even though there are times when you'd like to do this, it isn't healthy. Children need to learn to live with all the challenges that they're going to face. Nurturing faith on a daily basis is the best way to give them the tools they're going to need to do that.

Make your goal "worship plus two." Worship on a regular basis, and choose two other ways to connect to your church: Worship + Bible study + outreach, for instance. Or worship + fellowship + volunteering.

Worship is more than attendance at a one-hour church service. Worship is praise to the God in whom we "'live and move and have our being'" (Acts 17:28). Let that attitude guide the choices you make and the way you raise your children. Every time you let your faith inform your words and actions, you teach your child that living a life of faith is a full-time job, but one that you are glad to have.

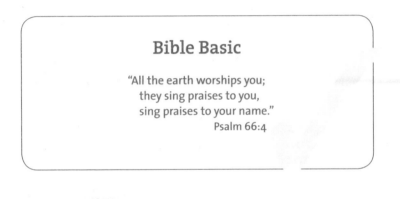

Bible Basic

"All the earth worships you;
they sing praises to you,
sing praises to your name."
Psalm 66:4

to be continued . . .

How did you live your faith outside of church this week?

19 Nurture your own spiritual life

One of the essential privileges of being a parent is putting your child first. One of the biggest drawbacks of being a parent is putting yourself last. This is true about our physical and emotional health; it is true of our spiritual health as well.

You teach your child to pray, but do you take time to pray on your own? You make sure your child is enrolled in a church school class, but do you attend an adult education course? You equip your kids with the latest version of the Bible in a language they can understand, but do you do the same for yourself? And if you do, do you take time to read it?

When it comes to living a spiritual life, the old adage "practice what you preach" was never more true. "Preparation to live with a face of faith in the world requires that adult Christians make intentional commitments to nurturing their faith—both individually and communally. Establishing regular patterns of spiritual formation, habits of mind and heart, have the power to feed hungry souls and form a face of faith that can meet the world with all of its demands and challenges."[10]

It is important to be involved in the faith activities that involve your children, but it is equally important to find places and opportunities that allow you to grow in faith. If you don't fill your own spiritual well with water, you won't be able to give a cup to your child, or to anyone else for that matter. Your own spirit needs tending, along with everyone else's. Nurturing your faith is a lifelong learning process. We don't graduate from the need to learn about God when we get our high school diploma.

It is not only necessary; it is fun! The Bible stories you learned as a child take on new meaning after you've had some experience with life. Discovering a new way of prayer is delightfully energizing. Learning a different spiritual practice—meditation, liturgical dance, walking a labyrinth—can lift you out of the spiritual doldrums. Try something you've wanted to do for a long time but never did: journaling, for instance. Fueling your own faith is a win-win situation for you and the rest of your family, too.

Being comfortable in your own faith allows children to be comfortable in theirs.

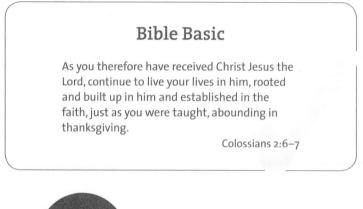

Bible Basic

As you therefore have received Christ Jesus the Lord, continue to live your lives in him, rooted and built up in him and established in the faith, just as you were taught, abounding in thanksgiving.

Colossians 2:6–7

to be continued . . . How much time per day do you spend tending to your spiritual needs?

20 *Embrace the mystery*

There is a great deal of mystery in faith. Children recognize this and aren't afraid of it. Somewhere along the way we squeeze the life out of faith and try to make it fit into a rational box where everything makes perfect sense. We forget that the mystery of God's love for us in Jesus Christ is just that—a mystery, an amazing one.

People of faith have tried to explain the details of theology for as long as the world has been around.

Allow room for the unanswerable, the unknowable aspect, the delightful mystery of life and faith.

In his book *Crossing the Desert*, Robert Wicks writes, "We must be willing to constantly sit on the edge of mystery and *un*learn what has helped guide us in the past but is no longer as useful now."[11] Relearning how to embrace the mystery of faith strengthens our spirit and brings us into the presence of God.

Children bring us into the mystery of God's presence. "The gift of being with children is that we have opportunities to hear perspectives on faith and God from those who are closer to those mysteries of birth and beginnings of life than we are," writes Christian educator Elizabeth Caldwell.[12] Young children who don't have a reason to distrust God bring a refreshing reminder of what it means to come before Jesus as a child. Children love God with a heart that is unencumbered with doubt and disappointment.

Don't squash the joy of mystery from your child's life. Curb the cynicism you may be prone to express. Think about how your negative words and actions affect your child's view of the world and of faith. If you are disillusioned with God, don't burden your child with your impressions. Try to see the world, and the events in your life, through a child's eyes.

Embrace the mystery of faith by embracing the mystery of life. Marvel at the miracle of creation. Listen to your child's bedtime prayers, the uninhibited beauty of them. Go for a walk with your child and, instead of being in a hurry to get someplace, watch as your child explores the mysteries of nature: the tilting dive of a butterfly, the tender pink of a budding flower, the thrill of a fresh breeze on a hot day.

Albert Einstein wrote, "The most beautiful experience we can have is the mysterious".[13]

Remember when you thought that you could catch a falling star? Maybe it's time to try that again.

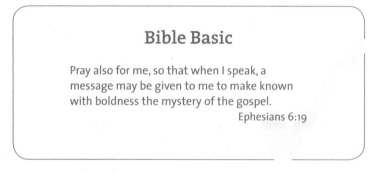

Bible Basic

Pray also for me, so that when I speak, a message may be given to me to make known with boldness the mystery of the gospel.

Ephesians 6:19

to be continued . . .

What mystery of faith is hardest for you to accept?

21 Remember when God became more than just a name to you

The "Quaker questions" are used as icebreakers when a group of people are getting to know one another. (What they have to do with Quakers is unknown.) New-member classes at church, small-group studies, even dinner gatherings enlist these questions as a way of getting the conversation going.

"How was your home heated as a child? In what room did the family most often gather? Who was the person to whom you went for warmth and comfort?" All the questions are good ones, but one in particular merits extra attention as you ponder ways to nurture your child's spiritual life: "When did God become more than just a name to you?"

Take your time answering the question. You may not be able to come up with an exact date or place or time; perhaps God always seemed personal and real to you. Can you think about a time when you took a step further along in your faith journey? Who encouraged you? What was the situation? What was frightening about this step, and what was invigorating?

Spiritual health is like any other kind of health. Sometimes our spirits are healthy, strong, and vital; sometimes our spirits are weak, frail, and weary. Look back over your life and remember these times.

You may discover that when your physical health was at a low point, your spirit was strong and kept you going. You may learn that your life has been peppered with doubts, but that never stopped you from believing in God. You may recall people who have been an essential part of your faith experience, people you haven't thought about in years.

Perhaps it is only recently that God became more than just a name to you. Maybe you're still waiting for that day to come.

Providing your children with the ways and means to have a healthy spirituality means continually striving for that in your own life. Put some thought into it. Share these thoughts with your children. You'll never have a more rapt audience than your children when they are young, eager to hear your stories over and over again.

Your story is part of your child's story, no matter what your faith background, no matter how long you've felt close to God, no matter if you are even now struggling to come to a new understanding of your relationship with the Almighty. Your story is part of your child's story, and both of your stories are part of God's unending story.

Bible Basic

Keep these words that I am commanding you today in your heart. Recite them to your children and talk about them when you are at home and when you are away, when you lie down and when you rise.

Deuteronomy 6:6–7

to be continued . . .

Who is the first person who ever talked to you about God?

22 *Find a church that welcomes children*

Church educator and author C. Ellis Nelson writes that "faith is communicated by a community of believers and . . . the meaning of faith is developed by its members out of their history, by their interaction with each other, and in relationship to the events that take place in their lives."[14]

Finding a church home where you and your child are welcome should be easy, but it's not always as simple as walking in the first church and discovering the perfect fit.

When you are searching for a church home, do some research so that you know the options in your area. Check the Yellow Pages of the phone book. Go for a drive and see what churches are nearby. Ask your friends and neighbors where they go to church. Start attending various churches on a Sunday morning and see how it feels, making sure you give each church a fair chance by attending more than once, unless you know for sure it isn't right for you.

A family with children needs a church home where children are welcome. Is there a child-care option during worship? What church school classes are available (for adults as well as for children)? Does someone welcome you when you come in the door? Do people make a point of talking to your child, not just to you? Does worship include a time set aside for a children's message? Are there children in worship throughout the service, or not at all?

Some families think it's a great idea to have church school and worship at the same time, making it possible for a family to come for one hour each week. The children attend church school while the parents attend worship, and everyone is finished at the same time. While this may sound convenient, the format doesn't lend itself to children becoming comfortable in worship, and it doesn't promote education for adults. If you want your children to be at home in worship and if you want to find a place where you can grow in your faith, find a format where worship and church school don't overlap.

If you think there are areas where your church could be more proactive in its ministry to children, speak up. Team up with the pastor or educator and brainstorm ideas. Visit other churches and find out what they're doing for children and what works for them. Volunteer to start a youth fellowship for middle-school kids if that is an area that is lacking. Don't be intimidated by small numbers; you can help build the group from the ground up. A church that doesn't have many kids in the middle-school age group but lots of kids of preschool age can become the church with a vital middle-school fellowship a few years down the road. Start with what you have, and then nurture the younger kids toward the time when they can become active in the middle-school group. Envision what your church can become, not just what it is.

Even if there aren't a lot of children, how they are perceived and welcomed will make an impact on your child. Parents tend to love the people who love their children, and that's exactly how a faith home should be.

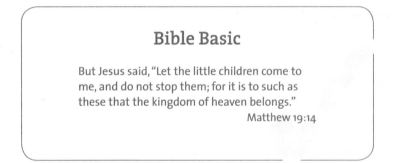

Bible Basic

But Jesus said, "Let the little children come to me, and do not stop them; for it is to such as these that the kingdom of heaven belongs."

Matthew 19:14

to be continued . . .

What is the most important aspect of a church for you?

23 *Keep the Sabbath*

Keeping the Sabbath doesn't mean you have to sit in a dark room all day. Keeping the Sabbath doesn't mean forbidding your family from playing cards and dancing. Keeping the Sabbath doesn't mean you have to be solemn and sad every Sunday; just the opposite, in fact.

Keeping the Sabbath means keeping time each week to rest from the usual rush of daily life; keeping a focus on God's involvement in your life; keeping your faith a priority, not just an occasional thing. The word "Sabbath" means "rest," and isn't that a welcome thought for busy families and exhausted parents!

Setting aside a Sabbath time has been part of our faith history since God created the world. After all of creation was complete, God took a day and rested, rejoicing in the heavens and the earth. As the Israelites traveled from slavery in Egypt back to their homeland, God insisted that they remember the Sabbath and take a day each week to rest and reenergize for the journey. Keeping the Sabbath is one of the Ten Commandments; that's how important it is.

There was a time (and perhaps it still happens in some places) when shops were closed, sports were suspended, and keeping the Sabbath might have been a bit easier to do. Nowadays, Sundays are as busy and full as any other day of the week. Still, we can find ways to keep the Sabbath, to set aside one day, or a portion of a day, to push away the clutter of life and rest in the joy of God.

Take a Sabbath break by not doing housework or cooking on Sundays. Prepare a meal the day before, or eat leftovers. If cooking a meal is fun and relaxing, then make it easy. Lots of people go out to brunch after church. If you can't afford to do this, make pancakes or waffles for Sunday dinner. Bake bread, and make that your meal, adding honey and peanut butter and a big bowl of fruit. Bake two loaves, and give one to a neighbor. Light special candles before you eat. Tell family stories.

Turn off the computer and go for a walk. Call the grandparents. Pile a stack of books in the living room and have a reading fest. Take naps. Sing songs. Spend as much time as you can relaxing together.

Keep the Sabbath as a day of centering on God, and take time for spiritual, physical, and emotional renewal. The rest of the week will fall into place much better if you do.

Bible Basic

Observe the sabbath day and keep it holy, as the LORD your God commanded you. Six days you shall labor and do all your work. But the seventh day is a sabbath to the LORD your God.

Deuteronomy. 5:12–14

to be continued . . .

What busyness or work can you put aside each week in order to keep the Sabbath?

24 *Have meals together*

For generations, the family dinner table has been the place where members gather together and catch up on one another's lives. It's not the only meal where this happens, but it tends to be the main one, with children eating lunch at school and parents working outside the home. Mornings are rushed enough getting everyone up, showered, fed, and out the door before the bus comes, let alone sitting at the breakfast table over a leisurely feast of something more substantial than cold cereal and toaster pastries.

Even families with the best intentions fall prey to the demise of the family dinner once their kids get involved in after-school programs. Fluctuating work schedules and evening meetings add to the many reasons why families spend less and less time eating a regular meal together.

Yet conversation, bonding, and sharing occur when people sit around the table and eat a meal. It's a shame to throw those valuable experiences out with the dishwater.

Eating a meal with loved ones is an essential element of our faith. The preparation and eating of meals was specifically spelled out in Old Testament times. Many holy days are feast days. In the New Testament, Jesus eats with Mary and Martha in their home. He feeds thousands of people after a long day of preaching, breaks bread with his disciples the night before his death, cooks fish for them on the beach after his resurrection. It is in the breaking of bread at the supper table that the two disciples recognize Jesus as the risen Lord after their journey to Emmaus. There is definitely something to glean from following Jesus' example of sitting at the table and sharing a meal with those who are most important to him.

In our fast-food, fast-track culture, this significant part of our family faith experience is neglected; we trade nutritious food and spiritual nourishment for empty calories and empty tables.

Life happens, and other activities get in the way of family time, but parents need to make every effort to gather the family around the table for a meal at least once a week. Schedule a family-night dinner on the calendar each week. This is sacred time, and nothing short of a crisis is to interfere with it. Plan to have a Saturday breakfast or Sunday brunch, if that suits your schedule better. You can alternate the day you choose, just be sure to choose one.

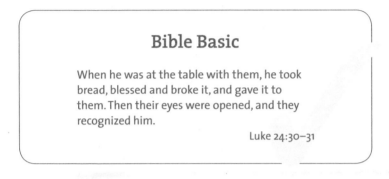

Bible Basic

When he was at the table with them, he took bread, blessed and broke it, and gave it to them. Then their eyes were opened, and they recognized him.

Luke 24:30–31

to be
continued . . .

What did your family dinner table look like when you were growing up? Is the table still in the family?

25 Admit that you don't have all the answers

Why do birds have wings? Why did God make ants? Why do people sleep? Why do cats purr? Why do I have to eat that? Why, why, why, why, *why*?

Why? Why is "why" the favorite question of young children and teenagers? Why? Because they are learning about themselves and the world, that's why.

Parents get tired of hearing the question "why?" We get tired because there is no end to the questions. We get tired because we think we have to answer every one of those questions.

We are tempted to say, "Because I said so!" but that isn't very helpful. Tempting, perhaps; but not helpful.

Parents, hear this! You don't have to have all the answers. In fact, the sooner you can believe this, the better. Let go of the guilt. You're not a bad parent if you don't answer every question your child asks. Nobody has all the answers. It is impossible.

Your child looks to you for guidance. Guidance means that you are supposed to help point that child in the right direction. If your child asks you a question and you're not sure of the answer, don't try to fake it. Say, "I'm not sure what that word means. Let's look it up in the dictionary." Let your child know that even if you don't have all the answers, you will help him discover the many resources that can provide the information you cannot.

If your child asks a question you're not ready to answer, say so. "I know you are curious about why we have to move to a new house. I need to think about that right now, but we can talk about it tonight after you're finished with your homework."

Try to understand the context of the question. Some questions arise from an immediate experience: "Why do my teeth hurt when I eat ice cream?" Some take days or weeks or months to formulate: "Why do you always cry when you talk about Grandma?" There's a difference. The first warrants a brief response, whereas the second may take more time, and the answer is probably multilayered as well.

Faith-based questions require extra patience and thought. "Why does God let people get sick?" reflects the child's quest to understand how God acts in the world and how we are to respond to what may seem unjust or cruel. You could even say to your child, "I ask myself the same question. What do you think? It makes us sad that Grandma is sick. But we love her whether she's healthy or sick, right? That's how God loves us."

John Westerhoff, a church educator, wrote that what "children are really asking is for us to reveal and share ourselves and our faith, not to provide dogmatic answers. We do not need to answer our children's questions, but we do need to make our faith available to them as a source for their learning and growth."[15]

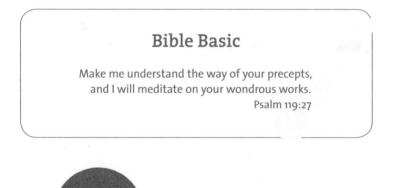

Bible Basic

Make me understand the way of your precepts,
and I will meditate on your wondrous works.

Psalm 119:27

to be continued . . . What question have you never been asked but wish you had?

26 *Share your highs and lows*

Would you like your time around the dinner table to be more than a synopsis of the family agenda or a chance to watch TV? Sharing your highs and lows is a wonderful way to connect with your family on more than a surface level. It's also a great way to get the conversation going, especially when your children get to the age when getting them to speak in more than grunts and sighs seems like a major effort.

Play the game of "High, Low, Whaddaya Know?" In this game nobody loses, and everyone gets the opportunity to take a turn.

Start with the oldest member of the family. Or the youngest. You make the rules.

The first person shares the high of the day. "I got an A on my math test!" The speaker gets to elaborate on why this is such a high. High fives all around! Now, the rest of the family takes a turn, each one sharing the high.

Next it's time to share the low. "I got stuck in traffic on the way home. That's a low for me because it means I have less time at home with all of you tonight." "My new friend got moved to a different class, and now I won't see him anymore." Again, everyone gets a turn.

After the highs and lows have been shared, it's time for "Whaddaya know?" Each family member shares something they learned that day, something they heard on the news, some piece of information they are eager to tell. No gossip allowed! The information shared should be something that has a little more benefit than telling tales on another person.

Some folks call this game "Roses and Thorns." The rose is the highlight of your day, and the thorn—you get the point. The title isn't what matters. Come up with one of your own if you'd like.

Another good question to add to the mix is "Where did you find God today?" "I found God in the neighbor who smiled and waved when I got off the bus." "I found God in the singing birds in the trees." "I found God in the hug I got from Daddy." Your family will be on the lookout for God in everyday events and people.

When family or friends gather at your dinner table, invite them to play the game with you. It's a good way to get to know your child's friends and engage them in the conversation. It might lead to this game being played at their family dinner table, too!

Bible Basic

Where can I go from your spirit?
  Or where can I flee from your presence?
If I ascend to heaven, you are there;
  if I make my bed in Sheol, you are there.
Psalm 139:7–8

to be continued . . .

What was the high point of your day? The low? Did you learn something new?

27 *Develop family rituals*

What family rituals were part of your childhood? Opening one present on Christmas Eve? Putting together a jigsaw puzzle on New Year's Day? Coloring eggs and hiding them around the house for the Easter afternoon egg hunt?

A ritual is an activity that is repeated regularly, often at the same time of the day or year. A daily ritual is a father kissing his daughter's forehead when he tucks her into bed each night. A yearly ritual is going for the first swim in the lake every Mother's Day.

Rituals provide consistency, connection, cohesion. Like anything repeated over and over, rituals become imprinted in us, in a good way. Rituals bind us to one another, even when family members are apart. They give us a sense of security and also of anticipation.

A lot of family rituals center around holiday traditions, but they need not be exclusive to that. Saying grace before meals, reading a bedtime story, writing a letter to Grandpa every Sunday evening—these family rituals are equally important.

Worship is ripe with rituals. Every Sunday, children light the candles on the Communion table. People pass the peace of Christ after the time of greeting. The collection of the offering always ends with a particular refrain of music. If those rituals suddenly came to a halt, we would feel off kilter. Rituals in worship are important for all ages, but for children, they may be the first part of worship that can be remembered and reenacted.

Family rituals connect us to faith rituals, which connect us to family rituals.

We may repeat the same rituals with which we grew up, and we may begin new ones with our own children. Most likely, we end up with a combination of the two. Think about the rituals that are regular practices for you now. Is there a ritual that could become part of your tradition? Don't be afraid to try something new. Find out what other families do. Bring some of the church rituals into your home. Lighting candles at the dinner table is easy, and it is a ritual that reminds the family of their faith home, where candles are lit each week as well. It may not make your dinnertime a worshipful event, but then again, it might be just the thing that does.

However busy our life may be, rituals bring something holy into that chaos.

Bible Basic

I commend you because you remember me in everything and maintain the traditions just as I handed them on to you.

1 Corinthians 11:2

Is there a family ritual from your childhood that you now reenact with your children?

28 *Create a Christian calendar*

Is there a busy family out there who can function without a calendar hung on the kitchen wall or in some place where it can't be missed? Chances are, that calendar is overflowing with appointments, events, holidays, deadlines, and reminders. Most families would be lost if they didn't have a calendar on which to coordinate and record their activities.

No matter how full your calendar is already, make room on it for the seasons of the church year, the holy days that give shape to our faith traditions. Better yet, start with a calendar that lists all the Christian seasons, and then fill in the rest of your activities around them.

The seasons in the church year revolve around the life, death, and resurrection of Jesus: Advent (the preparation for Jesus' birth); Christmas (the birth of Christ and the twelve days following); Epiphany (the visit of the wise magi, and the coming of the light of Christ into the world); Lent (the forty days of preparation for Jesus' passion and death); Holy Week (the events of the last week of Jesus' life, including Maundy Thursday and Good Friday); Easter (the resurrection of Jesus); Pentecost (the outpouring of the Holy Spirit on the fiftieth day after Easter and the birth of the Christian church); Ordinary Time (the remainder of the church year).

Christian educator Elizabeth Caldwell writes, "The seasons of the church year provide a framework for us to move through the story of the Christian faith as we learn and worship at church. Celebrating the seasons of the church year at home helps children make connections between beliefs and actions."[16] Posting the seasons of the church year in a visible place and framing the rest of your life around these seasons teaches your children that faith is a priority, not an afterthought.

Christmas comes on the same day every year, but Easter is determined by a lunar calendar. You may have to do a little research to discover the dates of all the church seasons, as they fluctuate from year to year. Their order in the church year, however, is steadfast.

Dates to include are Advent, Christmas, Epiphany, the Baptism of Jesus, Ash Wednesday, Lent, Maundy Thursday, Good Friday, Easter, Pentecost, World Communion Sunday, All Saints' Day. Plan to offer a special prayer on those days or play appropriate music or invite someone to share a small celebration. Connect your life to the church seasons. When you celebrate the day that is marked to remember the baptism of Jesus, share your own baptism stories.

The Christian year consists of more than Christmas and Easter, and it might be nice to celebrate a holy day that isn't nearly ruined by consumerism. Research how other cultures celebrate the holidays, and incorporate some new rituals into your usual celebrations.

Don't stop short by listing only Christian holy days. Include the special days of other faiths: Yom Kippur, Hanukkah, Ramadan. Creating such a calendar is a perfect way to teach tolerance and understanding of other faith traditions, even while you make a point of celebrating your own.

Bible Basic

I too decided, after investigating everything carefully from the very first, to write an orderly account for you.

Luke 1:3

to be continued . . .

What is your favorite holiday tradition?

29 *Let mistakes happen*

A first-grade classroom has a sign on the wall for everyone to see: "This is a place where mistakes and accidents can happen."

If children learned only that one lesson in first grade, it would set the stage for a lifetime of healthier attitudes, behavior, and interactions with other people.

If parents who never learned that lesson in first grade learned it as adults, that would be a huge relief for them, and for their children, too.

Children are going to make mistakes; we all do. That's life. And mistakes are not all bad.

We have a hard time watching our kids make mistakes. We want to protect them from anything that might hurt them, and we include mistakes in that category. *That* is a mistake.

Making mistakes allows us to learn forgiveness, to accept our own imperfections and those of others. It relieves the pressure of trying to be perfect all the time.

Let children make their own mistakes. You may want to protect them from making the same mistakes you made growing up, and that's understandable. Chances are, however, they will not only repeat the same mistakes you made but actually need to make them, to learn from them in their own way. When your child makes a mistake you warned him not to make, resist the temptation to say "I told you so."

When your children make mistakes, ask questions that will help them sort through things. "How will you do things differently the next time you're in this situation? What is the most important thing you learned from what just happened?"

It's OK for your children to see you make mistakes. They will learn how to accept imperfections in other people and in themselves. They will observe how you react when you make a mistake. Take some of the pressure off yourself by not trying to be perfect, and it will take some of the pressure off your children, too.

The Christian faith does not say we have to be perfect. Isn't that a relief? That's God's specialty, not ours.

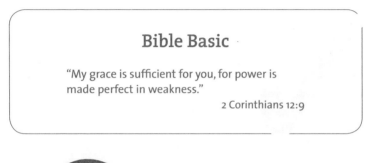

Bible Basic

"My grace is sufficient for you, for power is made perfect in weakness."

2 Corinthians 12:9

to be continued . . .

What mistake that you made helped you learn an important life lesson?

30 *Write a family table grace*

Multitudes of excellent books provide ready-made prayers and blessings for your use. That doesn't mean you can't write one of your own. Writing a family table grace is a great way to be intentional about how you think about God and to create an opportunity for all ages to become more comfortable with prayer.

Children are experts at spontaneous prayer. They can find all kinds of things for which to give thanks. "Thank you, God, for milk and bread and corn and chicken and napkins and . . ." Many a meal has grown cold while families wait patiently for their child to finish saying grace, or else they interject a quick "Amen!" before the gravy congeals on the mashed potatoes.

Grace before a meal is found in homes even if the families gathered around the table don't attend church. Kids seem to recognize at an early age the importance of offering a blessing or prayer when the family begins sharing a meal. In many homes, grace is the only prayer offered. That makes it all the more important.

You may have a table grace you learned as a child: "God is great, God is good; let us thank God for this food. Amen." Or "Rub-a-dub-dub, bring on the grub! Yay, God!" These graces sum up in a few short words the gist of prayer: the recognition of God's goodness and our gratitude for the blessings of our lives.

Make the process of writing a table grace the agenda for a family dinner. After your usual (or unusual) grace is offered, and while you are passing the food around, suggest that the family write their own, unique table grace. It doesn't have to rhyme, but it's certainly fine if it does. Listen to all the suggestions, and write them down. It may be a challenge to fit in everyone's ideas, but be sure that the final prayer has everyone's approval and that nobody's ideas are left out. If you can't come to an agreement, write a couple of table graces or have each child write his or her own. The more the merrier!

If your children approve, suggest sharing the table grace with your extended family the next time you're together, or offer it when you have a friend to dinner. Be sure your children are comfortable with this "public" recitation. They may prefer to keep the table grace private, and you don't want to step on tender toes.

Table grace doesn't have to be the same every time. Alternate using your family table grace, a favorite camp song, and a spontaneous prayer if that's what works for your family. The idea is not to be rigid, but to welcome all types of prayer.

It's not just the words that matter; what counts is the regular ritual of giving thanks to God as a family. The folding or holding of hands, the bowing of heads, the saying of a prayer are all important ingredients of a recipe that makes for a healthy family.

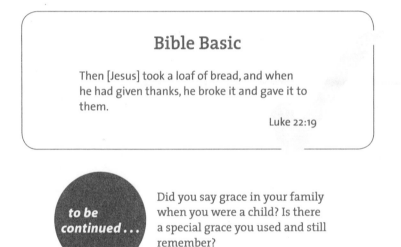

Bible Basic

Then [Jesus] took a loaf of bread, and when he had given thanks, he broke it and gave it to them.

Luke 22:19

to be continued . . .

Did you say grace in your family when you were a child? Is there a special grace you used and still remember?

31 *Use your imagination*

You don't have to be around children very long to realize that they have marvelous imaginations. Why do we have to lose that when we grow up? Why do we think that everything has to be reasonable, practical, and . . . boring?

How can we expect a child to imagine the vastness of God and the infinite possibilities of faith if we limit their—and our—imaginations? Words cannot confine the truths of the infinite; we cannot reduce the Trinity to a mere definition.

God has a wonderful imagination. Creating the heavens and earth out of nothing but chaos? Amazing! We need look no further than ourselves to realize that God has a great imagination. And what about armadillos and giraffes, rainbows and snow? What fun God must have had making everything from scratch, choosing shapes and colors and characteristics for everyone and everything.

The imagination of children is a gift we should cherish and try to reclaim for ourselves. Playing with children is a great exercise in stretching those stiff, neglected imagination muscles that somehow get forgotten when we become adults.

Play the "Imagine" game. Take turns asking the question, "Imagine if. . . ." and then adding something like ". . . our dog could talk. What would she say?" "Imagine if . . . we had wings and could fly anywhere we wanted to go. Where would you fly?" This is a great game to play in the car, on short or long rides, or on a rainy afternoon when you and your children are feeling a little stir crazy.

Take the attributes of different animals, put them together, and create something new. If you take the head of a rhinoceros, the body of an ostrich, and the tail of a lion, what do you get? A rhi-ostri-on!

You don't need a book to tell you how to use your imagination. Get down on the floor and have a tea party with your kids. Make the sofa into a magic carpet and sail off into the sky. Mix up a batch of miscellaneous ingredients and see what you get. It might not be edible, but it will be interesting.

Use your imagination. Your kids are the teachers now. And you? You are the very best student in the world!

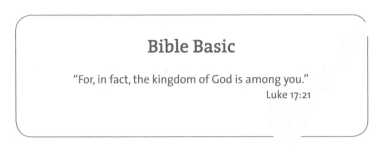

Bible Basic

"For, in fact, the kingdom of God is among you."

Luke 17:21

to be continued . . . Imagine if . . . you could have the power of a superhero. What would it be?

32 Design a family coat of arms

A coat of arms isn't some strange piece of winter attire. It is a pictorial symbol of a family's history.

The tradition of a family coat of arms can be traced back to early times in many countries. A coat of arms was often associated with medieval times, as a means of identifying rival soldiers. There had to be some quick way to let the guys under those suits of armor know who was on the other horse.

One of the most important uses of a coat of arms is to indicate the relationship of family members to one another. Although you may be able to research your historical coat of arms, creating a new one can be an ideal way to talk through the unique traits of your family, as well as to embrace and celebrate the history and traditions that help shape the ways in which you understand and express your faith.

Brainstorm a variety of options that might be used as illustrations on your coat of arms. What foods represent your ethnic traditions? What places have you visited that have significance for your family (for example, a favorite vacation spot)? Are there particular animals, or animal characteristics, that have meaning for you? Gather photographs of family celebrations, such as baptisms and birthdays.

Use scratch paper to design your shield, and when you're ready, take a sheet of heavy paper or cardboard and draw the outline of a shape: a circle, oval, square, any shape will do. Combine several shapes if you wish.

You aren't limited to four categories, but dividing your coat of arms into sections is a good way to focus on what you want to be represented in your final design.

Use your own sketches, computer graphics, and photos (or words—your own or those cut from a magazine) and arrange these on the coat of arms. Take your time. You may decide to rearrange the designs before pasting them on permanently.

Each family member can create his or her own coat of arms, but have one symbol (the cross, for instance) that is the same in each of them.

Hang the coat of arms where it is visible to others. This is an excellent way to share your faith stories with those who come into your home.

Make T-shirts using the coat of arms. You can buy iron-on or computer-transfer paper and print the design from your own computer.

If you're not comfortable using the symbolism of a coat of arms, design a flag instead.

Bible Basic

The Lord is my strength and my shield;
in him my heart trusts.

Psalm 28:7a

to be continued . . .

In what ways do you feel most protected by God?

33 Encourage questions

Children are great ones for asking questions. Asking questions and seeking answers is how we learn about the world. It's one way we keep growing in our faith, no matter how old we are.

Parents sometimes discourage questions when they don't know, or don't like, the answers.

Even though you don't have all the answers, encourage the questions.

Don't go overboard in the other direction either, by answering much more than your child is asking. When a four-year-old asks, "Where do babies come from?" he might not be expecting a full explanation of reproductive biology. Chances are, he saw the neighbor unloading her new baby from the car for the first time and wonders if babies come from the grocery store.

Learn to understand the questions behind the questions. What is the child really asking? Try to understand the question from the child's point of view, which may be different from your own.

At different ages, children have different reasons for asking the questions they ask. Rabbi Harold Kushner suggests that when a very young child asks, "Is there really a God?" that question actually stems from a child's concern about the stability and security of the world. When a teenager asks the same question, issues of limitations, of justice and unfairness, may be at the core.[17]

Jean Piaget, a Swiss psychologist well known for his expertise in child psychology, taught that the questions of young children tend to be functional rather than theoretical. Children seek to understand the world and how it applies to them. Children are constantly trying to figure out how their experiences have meaning for them.

Think of questions as opportunities to explore faith with your child. "Why did God make vegetables?" can lead to a discussion about all the many wonderful things God made in the world at the beginning of time. When your child asks, "Why did Grandpa die?" you have the opportunity to talk to your child about heaven. Your child may also be worrying about the fact that you might die, too; you can reassure her that you plan to live for a long time and that, no matter what, you will be sure that she is never alone in the world, that there will always be people to help take care of her.

The poet Rainer Maria Rilke wrote, "Be patient toward all that is unsolved in your heart and try to love the questions themselves."[18] Love the questions that your children ask. Love the questions that remain unanswered. Love the questions that lead you to a deeper understanding of God.

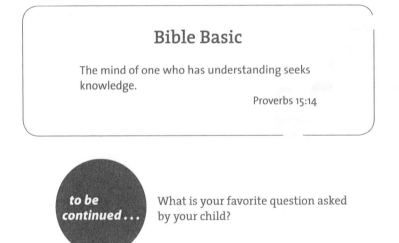

Bible Basic

The mind of one who has understanding seeks knowledge.

Proverbs 15:14

to be continued... What is your favorite question asked by your child?

34 *Talk about death and dying*

We dread talking to our children about two topics: sex and death. Both are part of the natural order of things, yet we'd like to pretend that neither one exists, especially when we think of our children.

Death is part of the natural order of life. None of us gets out of this world alive. But death is also a terrifying termination of what we know.

Death is a primary component of the Christian faith. Jesus died, but we know that wasn't the end for him. Death isn't the end for us either; at least not in the long run. It is, however, the end of life as we know it, and that leaves us with questions and fear.

At some point in your children's lives, they will experience the death of someone they know or someone they love. It could be a family pet, a grandparent, a neighbor, a classmate, a sibling, a parent. Talking to your children about death before it happens makes it less scary when it does. Imagine how frightening it is for a child to know nothing about death and then to suddenly be told that a playmate has died and that the child will never see her again. You may think it is best to wait until a child must hear about death before you talk about it, but then the emotions and sorrow of a particular death are tangled up with the telling, and it makes things even more complicated.

If you are uncomfortable talking about death and don't know where to begin, check your church or library or bookstore for children's storybooks in which someone dies. Reading a story with your child opens the way for conversation. A story about the death of a beloved grandmother or a pet brings up the subject in a natural, loving way. You may not even finish the story before your child starts to ask you questions. That's fine. Listen to the questions as the child asks, and answer as best as you can.

Lent and Easter provide a perfect opportunity to talk about dying and death. As children hear the story of Jesus' death and resurrection year after year, it becomes obvious that death is not only part of life, it is part of our faith.

Talking about death can provide a natural venue for talking about resurrection. There is a life beyond this one, a life where everything is as it should be. We will be with God there, and nobody will ever be sad again. The promise of resurrection is what gives us hope as Christian people. Your child ought to know that, right from the start.

Bible Basic

"Do not let your hearts be troubled. Believe in God, believe also in me. In my Father's house there are many dwelling places.... I will come again and will take you to myself, so that where I am, there you may be also."

John 14:1–3

to be continued...

How did you first experience the reality of death?

35 *Respond to current events from a faith perspective*

Nurturing your children's spiritual health does not mean keeping them ignorant about the world around them. Certainly, there are exceptions to this. Letting your four-year-old watch the news with graphic depictions of the violence of war will be more traumatic than enlightening.

However, even young children need to know that their faith in God is not separate from their interactions with others, nor from the tragedies that seem so pervasive. Faith equips your child to face the world, not fear it.

Children are incredibly perceptive and pick up quickly on what's happening in the larger world. They catch glimpses of news on TV or the Internet, overhear people talking, and, once they can read, are apt to glance at more than the comics when they pick up a newspaper.

Children are very sensitive to your emotions, too. If you are upset because you just read on the Internet about a tornado that touched down in the next county, your children are going to sense this. They will be much more uneasy about what they don't know than what they do, especially if parents are trying to cover up bad news, so be honest about what has happened and why you are upset. Let your child ask questions. Pray together.

Children have plenty of good reasons to feel helpless, because they depend on adults for so many things. Empower your children in concrete ways. Feeling helpless isn't the answer. Finding ways to be helpful may be, at least in part.

The tragedies in the world are not the result of a wrathful God seeking to destroy creation. The Gospels show Jesus reaching out over and over again to the poor, the homeless, the sick, the needy. You can do the same. Take your child to the grocery store, and buy a couple of bags of food to feed the people whose homes were destroyed by the tornado you read about. Write letters to soldiers far from home. Collect coins from neighbors and friends to give to a charity that is asking for donations to help a local child fight cancer.

Theologian Karl Barth said that we should approach life with the Bible in one hand and a newspaper in the other. This is how we live a faithful life: by embracing the world as God does; by serving Christ as we serve one another.

Bible Basic

I will bring my knowledge from far away,
and ascribe righteousness to my Maker.

Job 36:3

to be continued . . .

What recent news event made you think about your faith and how you live what you believe?

36 *Make an Advent chain*

An Advent chain is not a new idea. The original use of an Advent chain was to help children count down the days from the first Sunday of Advent until Christmas Eve. Each day, one of the chain's twenty-four links is removed, providing a visual answer to the question "how many more days until Christmas?"

Here is a new idea for an Advent chain: Instead of removing links, add to the chain day by day, so that you have a finished chain when Christmas arrives. More than that, each link in the chain provides an activity for the day, and the activities include ways to nurture your faith and to reach out to others in the true spirit of Christmas.

Make a list from one through twenty-four. Divide the list into three sections of eight. Each section has a theme: events to enjoy as a family; faith-based fun; outreach to other people.

Brainstorm together to come up with your list. Under "events to enjoy as a family," give each family member a special day, when that person gets to choose what's for dinner, and another activity to be enjoyed by all the family: a game, a movie, and so on. For "faith-based fun," include reading the story of Christmas from Luke and singing a Christmas song. For "outreach to other people," think of ways you can be kind to someone else: bake cookies for a neighbor, invite a church friend over for dinner, call someone you love. By dividing the list into the three categories, you'll have a well-rounded holiday countdown that ensures some quality family time, while keeping an outward focus as well.

Cut twenty-four strips of paper, in whatever colors your family chooses. On each strip of paper, write down a different item from your list. Toss the links into a basket.

On the first day of Advent, the youngest member of the family gets to choose a link. You might want to do this first thing in the morning so that everybody can anticipate what's coming and so that you can provide yourself the time you may need to prepare for baking cookies (or running to the store to buy some ready-made treats). At the end of the first day, start your chain by making a loop with the link, stapling it together, and hanging it on the tree. It may look kind of pathetic for a while, but the chain will grow as the days go by, just as our faith is meant to grow as we practice the living of it each and every day.

Bible Basic

In all this I have given you an example that by such work we must support the weak, remembering the words of the Lord Jesus, for he himself said, "It is more blessed to give than to receive."

Acts 20:35

to be continued . . . What holiday tradition is dearest to your heart?

37 *Let children work out their disagreements*

It's tempting for parents to think that they are supposed to referee their kids every time there is a fight or disagreement. Children need to learn how to handle interactions with others without parents stepping in all the time. You can't fix everything, and besides, children learn important skills and confidence when they solve difficult problems by themselves.

Let your kids figure out ways to negotiate their disagreements. You can't always be the one in the striped shirt blowing the whistle, although there are situations when a time-out for both sides is in order. Solving an altercation when it is at its peak doesn't always work very well, and there may need to be a cooling-off period. After the opposing teams have calmed down a bit, let them know they need to figure out what caused the dispute, how they are going to deal with it, and what they can do differently next time to avoid the problem altogether.

Avoid taking sides. Kids will try to get you on their side, for obvious reasons. If you didn't see the conflict start and the reasons for it, you don't have all the facts and can't make a fair decision about who was right and who was wrong. Tell them, "you work it out."

Discourage your children from becoming tattletales. Tattletales want to make themselves look good and to gain the upper hand in a disagreement by pulling in the "big guns"— the parents. If you respond to the tattletale by punishing the child who is being tattled on, the tattletale gets the message that tattling works.

There's a difference between tattling and bringing important information to your attention. When your child comes to you with the news that "Johnny turned on the TV when you said not to," that's tattling. Children do not need to constantly inform the parent how the other kids are misbehaving. However, when your child runs to you and announces that "the baby is eating the dog food!" that's a situation in which you need to offer a response (unless you don't mind if your baby and your dog share a bowl of kibble).

Step in when there is threat of physical violence or when one child is bullying another. A small or docile child may need protection from a large or more aggressive one. Physical abuse is never an appropriate answer to a disagreement.

Practice negotiating skills when there is not a conflict in progress. Take a past situation in which tempers flared or come up with an imaginary scenario. Have the children reverse roles so that they can understand how it feels to be in the other person's shoes. Suggest that they write a list of possible ways to handle their disagreements in the future. If they help decide the rules, they will be more likely to follow them.

And as is true in nearly every case, your children learn by watching you work out disagreements with other adults. If you stalk off and slam the door when you don't get your way, don't be surprised if your children practice the same tactics.

Bible Basic

"So when you are offering your gift at the altar, if you remember that your brother or sister has something against you, leave your gift there before the altar and go; first be reconciled to your brother or sister, and then come and offer your gift."

Matthew 5:23–24

to be continued . . .

How did your family handle disagreements when you were growing up? How has that affected the way you handle disagreements as an adult?

38 Write a family creed

From time to time in the history of the church, the basic beliefs of the faith have been summarized in a creed, a succinct statement of the doctrines and principles of a religious system or denomination. The word "creed" comes from the Latin word *credo,* which means "I believe." The Apostles' Creed and the Nicene Creed are two of the best-known creeds, often recited in worship.

Families have their own creeds, although they may not be written out as such. These creeds include basic fundamentals upon which the family carries out its daily tasks and interactions. A family creed may fall into place without a lot of thought. Who gets the first shower in the morning may have more to do with who has to get out the door first or who is the earliest riser, than it does with anything else.

Taking time to identify what makes your family unique, and how you function as a team, can enhance your family's sense of worth and well-being. A fun way to do this is to write your own family creed in which you state the things that you believe are essential to the spiritual and emotional health of your family.

Post a sheet of paper where everyone can reach it. At the top of the paper, write, "We believe . . ." Brainstorm together, writing down the first thoughts that come to mind. Some prompts to get you started:

> If you had one word to describe your family, what would it be?
> How is each of you unique?
> What is your favorite thing to do as a family?
> What are the rules, and which can be broken and which cannot?
> How do you express your family's faith beliefs?

Let the ideas sit for a while, then go back to them. Leave the paper posted so that family members can add items on their own as they think of them.

After a week or two, gather together and prioritize the list by numbering the items, but don't be too rigid. If you have several items of equal ranking, don't feel as though you have to pick one over the other. The prioritizing is simply a way to help put the items in a format to be written down as a family creed.

Finally, take the list and write out your creed on a clean piece of paper or posterboard. Post it in a visible location.

As the family changes and grows, rewrite parts of the creed that need to be altered. Invite other family members (grandparents, for instance) to add to the creed. Use the creed as a family prayer.

Bible Basic

"As for me and my household, we will serve the LORD."

Joshua 24:15

to be
continued . . .

How does your family's creed compare to the beliefs in which you were raised?

39 *Teach tithing*

The idea of tithing comes from the Bible. The actual word, "tithe," is derived from an Old English word that means "tenth."

The Old Testament spells out the requirement that the people give 10 percent of everything they had to God, to support the priests and to keep the people mindful of all that God had given to them (see Leviticus 27:30–32; 2 Chronicles 31:5). This included livestock, produce, lamp oil, wine, money—*everything*. These "first fruits," as they came to be called, were to be the very best of what the people had, not the dregs.

The New Testament carries on the concept of tithing, although a percentage amount is not specifically mentioned. Paul encourages the new Christians to give according to their means: "For if the eagerness is there, the gift is acceptable according to what one has—not according to what one does not have.... It is a question of a fair balance between your present abundance and their need, so that their abundance may be for your need, in order that there may be a fair balance" (2 Corinthians 8:12–14).

Teaching your children to tithe should begin as soon as they have money. Show them the importance of setting aside their contribution when they receive their allowance or a gift of money, not after they have spent what they wanted. This is a good rule of thumb for adults, too.

Take three envelopes; mark one for church, one for spending, one for saving. Using a dollar as a point of reference, your child places ten cents in the church envelope first. You can decide with your child how the remaining amount of the money is to be divided between spending and saving.

If your church provides offering envelopes for children, use these to bring the tithe to worship. If you do not have preprinted offering envelopes, your child can design one using an ordinary small envelope, with the child's name and the date written on it. A crayon-colored, illustrated envelope in the offering plate makes for a cheerful offering for those giving and for those receiving.

Think about tithing not only your money, but also your time. Designate a certain number of hours per month for charity work or volunteer work at church (time in worship does not count). Let your child be involved in these activities as part of his or her giving (see entry 14).

Whatever you give—time, talents, income—give with a joyful heart, not reluctantly or grudgingly. It is a privilege to give to God's work on earth.

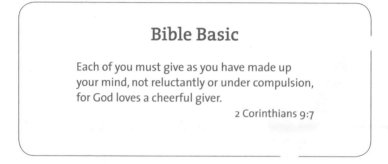

Bible Basic

Each of you must give as you have made up your mind, not reluctantly or under compulsion, for God loves a cheerful giver.

2 Corinthians 9:7

to be continued . . .

What percentage of your income do you give to church and charity work?

40 *Laugh often and much*

Laughter should be a major component of anyone's health plan. It doesn't cost you or your insurance company any money, can actually save relationships, and pays high premiums for all who get their daily dose.

The deep-bellied, unabashed laughter of an infant makes even the hard-hearted among us loosen up and smile. An older adult's face that has settled into a perpetual smile is the sign of someone who has dealt well with life. Make it a goal to be one of those adults.

Families should be filled with laughter. You and your children can have fun laughing together, and other people will want to be with you if you're known for being a family who laughs together.

Exercise your smile muscles. Stand in front of a mirror and observe the muscles you use smiling and frowning. See what you look like in both instances and decide how you'd rather have others see you.

Try to make each other laugh. See who can make the goofiest face or tell the silliest joke. Take pictures of yourselves being goofy and put them on your refrigerator, mirrors, and doors, so you'll be reminded of the fun at moments when you may need a laugh (such as heading out the door for a big test at school).

Read the comics in the newspaper together. Even children who are too young to read can appreciate a funny cartoon.

Go out and do something fun. Play miniature golf, spend an afternoon at the zoo, go out for ice cream.

Bring laughter into your home frequently, especially when your family is undergoing stress or trauma. Watch funny movies and read funny books.

Spend time with people who make you laugh.

You may get tired of seeing toys all over your house, but they are a sign that playful times are happening within your home. Once your children are beyond the age of toys, keep a few toys around where you can see them, and play with them every now and then. We should never get too old to play, to build with blocks or paint with our fingers.

Keep things in perspective. If you catch yourself being too serious, ask yourself, "Is this a situation worth being upset about? Can I do something to change it?" If you can lighten up, then do it, and save the serious side for those times when you really need it.

Families may look back over their lives and wish that they had laughed more. Few look back and wish they had laughed less.

Laughter truly is the best medicine. Laughter boosts the immune system, helps people breathe better, lowers blood pressure, massages the heart and other internal organs, and improves creativity and memory. Besides, it feels good to let loose with a hearty laugh now and then.

Bible Basic

But let the righteous be joyful;
let them exult before God;
let them be jubilant with joy.
Psalm 68:3

to be continued . . .

When was the last time you laughed so hard you cried?

41 *Choose your battles*

Every Sunday morning it's the same story. Your ten-year-old son loves to come to church but chafes at wearing the clothes you insist on. He wants to wear sweatpants, his usual choice. You were raised in a family that dressed up for church, and you believe that it is important for everyone to wear nicer clothes on Sunday morning. By the time you get to church, you and your son, and the rest of the family, are in a terrible mood from the ongoing arguments about church attire.

Is this the battle you want to fight each week? What really matters—that your son loves to come to church and is happy to do so in his sweatpants or that he dresses as you wish and you both end up miserable?

Some battles are worth fighting, and some simply are not. There will be plenty of opportunities to butt heads with your child, so you might as well learn to be choosy. Of course, there are times when you have to stand your ground because the safety and well-being of your child demands it. But if there's a possibility you can let a battle go, then let it go.

Next time you and your child end up in a battle of the wills, ask yourself a few simple questions:

> Why does this matter so much to me?
> Is my child's choice putting her safety at risk?
> Do I have to win every argument?
> What is the end result of my getting my way?
> What happens if I let it go?
> What am I teaching my child by insisting that my choices are always the best ones?
> Project yourself forward about five years, as if you are looking back on your current battle with your child. Will it really matter then that you get the final say now? Or will you wish you had let it go?

It may help to get away from thinking that one of you has to win and one of you has to lose. Instead, find a compromise that is acceptable to both of you. You can have differing opinions without one opinion being better than the other.

Children learn cooperation by knowing that their points of view are valid and that you take them seriously. Even if your decision is the one that ends up being enforced, the fact that you listened to your child and tried to understand the reasoning behind his or her opinion allows for more open and satisfying communication. Perhaps your son wants to wear sweatpants to church for the purely practical reason that he's super skinny and he feels much more comfortable in sweatpants than dress slacks that don't fit right. Find out the reasons for his choices. Even if you don't agree, don't belittle the rationale.

You realize that lots of parents would be delighted if their son loved to come to church as much as yours does. "OK," you tell him, "you can wear sweatpants to church. But they need to be clean, with the knees still intact. Deal?" Deal!

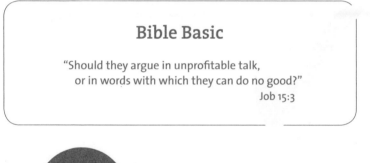

Bible Basic

"Should they argue in unprofitable talk,
    or in words with which they can do no good?"
                                                Job 15:3

to be continued . . .

What battle are you fighting now?
What would happen if you let it go?

42 *Ask for help*

A parent must be a maid, chef, taxi driver, conflict manager, economist, nurse, confidante, friend, mind reader—with no pay and little sleep. And you're reluctant to ask for a little help now and then?

If you are a single parent and your child's other parent is absent or uninvolved, you end up trying to be both mother and father. There is probably no tougher job in the world.

One of the first things to accept as you undertake the challenges and joys that come with being a parent is that you don't have to do it all yourself. It's OK to ask for help; in fact, it is necessary for your and your child's well-being and mental health. It's good for your children to have people besides you in their lives.

Enlist family and friends to watch the kids so that you get a break now and then. Ask friends or pastors to recommend people who can be trusted to watch your children. Exchange child-care duties with other parents; you watch their kids for a day and they return the favor.

Invite other trusted adults to be active participants in your child's upbringing. Your teenager will benefit from knowing that there are other adults who care about him and enjoy spending time with him. Try not to be jealous when your child confides in someone other than you; and don't take it personally, even if it is personal. Be grateful that your child trusts another adult and has an outlet for concerns.

If your child needs extra help with schoolwork, hire a tutor or ask the school if there is a teacher or mentor who can help. This could save a great deal of frustration for you and for your child. Children often learn better from someone other than their parent anyway, so it only makes sense to make use of people who are trained in skills you might not have.

Take a class on parenting at your church or local college. It helps to know what is typical behavior for a particular age and what merits extra attention. Talk to other parents and find out how they handle their problems and frustrations, but also celebrate with one another how you are a good parent and what you feel you've done right. Applaud one another's efforts. A little affirmation goes a long way.

Have your own interests and take time for yourself. You're setting a good example for your child to learn to do the same, and you refuel your gas tank so that you get better mileage out of your parenting energy and resources.

Parenting is a job where being the body of Christ makes a lot of sense. We can't be eyes and ears and hands and feet and voices and hearts and do it all well all the time. Embrace the gifts and outreach of other people and accept their help as a gift of grace.

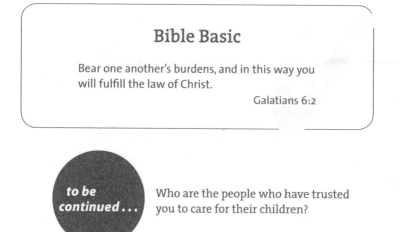

Bible Basic

Bear one another's burdens, and in this way you will fulfill the law of Christ.

Galatians 6:2

to be continued . . .   Who are the people who have trusted you to care for their children?

43 *Teach and practice conflict management*

The Bible tells us that one day the lion and the lamb will lie down together and everyone will live in peace. Until that day comes, we are going to have to deal with conflict.

Some people seem to thrive on conflict, and others avoid it at all costs. Teaching and practicing conflict management helps your child deal with both types, while avoiding the danger of becoming either extreme.

When we learn to resolve conflicts within a family where we are loved and respected, it results in respect and compassion. Put a few of these tools in your child's conflict resolution tool belt and sharpen your own skills while you're at it:

- Handle small concerns before they escalate. Piling up conflicts makes the resolution far more complicated.
- Keep your voice calm when you can. An angry tone ignites more conflict; a calm one eases the tension and allows both sides to settle down.
- Take a breath or two. The old adage about counting to ten before you say something is good advice.
- If the conflict cannot be resolved when it occurs, give it a little time. Agree to talk when both sides are calmer.
- Don't put off the resolution indefinitely, just temporarily. Giving some space may lead to a truer resolution.
- Let both sides speak. Conflict can be a result of a misunderstanding. Listening to how the other person feels, or why he reacted with anger, helps that person feel respected, and helps you understand what went wrong.
- Don't back the other person into a corner with threats and accusations. The reaction of someone in a corner is to fight, not to back down.
- Deal with conflict and seek resolution. This leads to appreciation of other people's opinions and differences.
- Avoid sweeping conflicts under the rug because it seems easier than dealing with them. You'll end up tripping over all the lumps in the rug eventually if you do.
- Allow your children to disagree with you in a respectful way. Children who always have to give in because the

adults are never wrong do not learn how to handle conflict, nor to speak up for themselves when they ought to do so.

- Do not let people bully you into a fight or a compromise.

We can control only how we act and respond. We cannot control the actions or response of another person.

If all your attempts at conflict resolution fail, know that you've given it your best shot. Know when to step away and let it go. It doesn't mean you are a failure

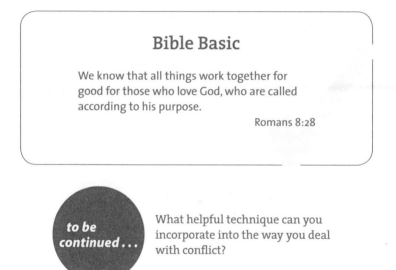

Bible Basic

We know that all things work together for good for those who love God, who are called according to his purpose.

Romans 8:28

to be continued . . .   What helpful technique can you incorporate into the way you deal with conflict?

44 *Nurture the environment*

A little girl asked her father, "Are God and Mother Earth married?"

The father thought for a moment. "No," he said. "They're just good friends."

We are Mother Earth's friends, too. Are we good friends or bad friends? That's a question we all need to ask.

Read the first chapter of the book of Genesis. We see God forming creation out of chaos and, with great imagination and love, birthing a beautiful world. God charges us with the stewardship, or care, of this world. From the moment people take their first breath, the world is in their hands.

Nurturing the environment, being stewards of the earth, is a responsibility in which all ages can participate. Start at home, and then branch out.

Teach children water conservation. Don't let the water run and run when you're washing your face or brushing your teeth. Fill the bathtub only with the water you need to get clean. Turn off lights when you're not in a room. Keep water bottles in the refrigerator for each family member, so there is less likelihood of running faucets. Pack lunches with reusable containers, to cut back on garbage. Use lunch boxes or cloth lunch bags. Use scrap paper for drawing, and don't forget to use both sides of the paper.

Make it a game. "Who gets to come with me and make sure the lights are turned off? Let's see how many dishes we can fit in the dishwasher! Time to fill the water bottles before we go to bed, so we'll all have fresh water in the morning!"

Plant a garden, even an herb garden in your kitchen window. Marvel at the way seeds turn into plants that yield beautiful flowers or wonderful things to eat.

Set up a recycling center in your garage and teach your children what items go in the different containers. Children can be in charge of gathering up newspapers, rinsing out empty cans, putting the recycling bins at the curb.

It should go without saying: do not litter! But judging by the amount of litter everywhere, some folks aren't listening. Do not litter, and teach your children why littering is harmful to God's earth. If you're at the playground and you see other people's litter, pick it up and throw it away. Again, make this into a game. Bring paper bags to the park, and garden gloves, and see who can pick up the most trash. Be careful if there is glass or rusty metal. Picking up anything that might be dangerous can be your job. Kids can focus on paper trash; there's plenty of that!

Make time to enjoy the great outdoors. Cherishing the beauty of God's earth makes us all the more eager to protect that beauty. Be a friend of Mother Earth. She can use all the friends she can get.

Bible Basic

God saw everything that he had made, and indeed, it was very good.

Genesis 1:31

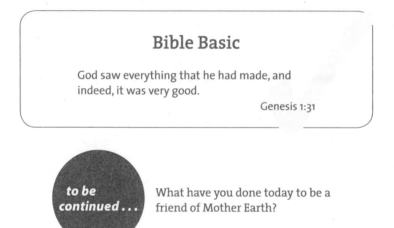

to be continued . . . What have you done today to be a friend of Mother Earth?

45 *Take care of yourself*

When you fly in an airplane, basic safety rules are explained and enforced. Fasten your seat belt. Put the tray table in the upright position. If there is a change in cabin pressure, oxygen masks will pop from the ceiling above you. *Make sure you secure your own mask before you attempt to help anyone else.* That goes for your health, whether or not you travel. Take care of yourself! It is vital.

There are plenty of times when your child's health comes before your own. If you need to take a sick child to the doctor, you might have to cancel the exercise class you had planned to take that day. Life happens. That's all the more reason to take good care of yourself on a regular basis, so that you can have the health and strength you need when your children need you. Your body is the temple of the Holy Spirit, remember? Treat it as such.

If you don't have a primary care physician, find one. Talk to friends or your pastor to get recommendations. Get an annual checkup. If you have a doctor you like and trust and see on a regular basis, you'll be more inclined to call the doctor if you have a question or health concern. You may be able to avoid more serious health conditions if you keep a close watch on your overall health.

Be thoughtful about what you eat. You make sure your kids eat a balanced diet, so why do you skip meals or overindulge late at night? Your children are more aware of what you eat, or don't eat, than you may think. Stock your shelves and refrigerator with snacks that are good for you, as well as for your children. Drink water and save soda for a special occasion. Splurge now and then with a special treat. You'll be less likely to crave stuff that isn't healthy if you allow yourself to have an occasional indulgence.

Exercise! Playing with your kids is a great way to make sure you have some physical activity beyond walking to the car. Go to the park, swing on the swings, play freeze tag, get out that hula hoop. Trying to keep up with children is good for your heart in more ways than one.

Choose a physical activity that is separate from your children. Take a yoga class, or go for a brisk walk with a friend or by yourself several times a week. If your kids see you exercising for the fun of it, they won't grow up thinking that exercise is something to avoid.

Perhaps the most difficult piece in caring for your health is to get enough sleep. There are times in your life (think newborn baby) when it is impossible. Still, make every effort to get your rest. Give up the hour you spend surfing the Internet and add that hour to your nightly sleep. Your body will thank you in the morning.

Bible Basic

Do you not know that you are God's temple and that God's Spirit dwells in you? . . . For God's temple is holy, and you are that temple.

1 Corinthians 3:16, 17b

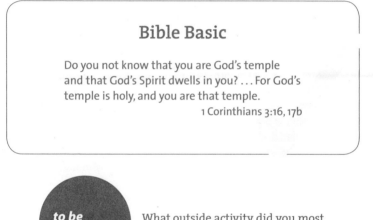

to be continued . . .

What outside activity did you most enjoy when you were a child? Now?

46 *Cherish individuality*

In the late 1960s, the comedy team of brothers Tom and Dick Smothers got a lot of mileage out of Tom's whining to Dick that "Mom always did like you best." People laughed at the way Tom deadpanned that line; but sadly that comment hits too close to home for too many people.

No matter how hard you try to be fair, your children will find reasons to think you favor one child over another. It's inevitable that on any given day, one member of the family will get more attention than another. A few of the following ideas may help each child feel valued. Along with these tips, think about who and what made you feel special as a child, and why.

Realize that each family member will have different reactions to the same situation. There's not a right and a wrong way to express grief, joy, frustration. Some children close off when they're sad, and others have to work it out by throwing themselves into activity. Respect and honor each individual's way of expression.

Give children responsibilities. When children feel that their contributions are important to the well-being of the family, it increases their self-worth.

If you have more than one child, each parent should have one-on-one time with each child. Let the child choose how you're going to spend an afternoon together, even if it means snuggling on the couch watching a movie. Give your full attention to the child you're with.

Give equal time to those things that interest each child. You may love sports and be thrilled to attend your daughter's ten thousand annual soccer games. Your son, who prefers to curl up and read, needs to have you read along with him. Don't make a bigger deal out of one child's activities than the other's.

Praise the efforts, not just the results. One child gets straight As without even trying, while the other works extra hard just to pull Bs. Good grades are nice, but the effort a child makes should be acknowledged more than the outcome.

Avoid making comparisons. "Jen's hair is always combed and neat. Why can't you wear your hair that way?" The opposite response isn't helpful, either. "You are so much prettier than anyone else in your class!" Comments like that put too much pressure on kids and set them up to compare themselves to others all the time.

Post a photograph of each family member on separate sheets of paper, and identify what makes each person unique and special. Include physical characteristics: eye color, hair, freckles, and so on. List the person's favorites: color, food, book, activity. Add to the information—your own and one another's—as new ideas arise.

People are like snowflakes. No two are exactly alike. God loves each person individually and equally. The Bible tells us so!

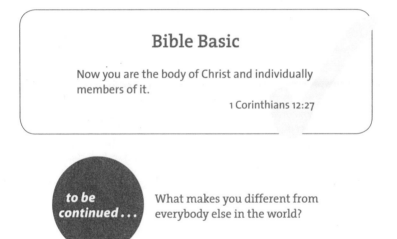

Bible Basic

Now you are the body of Christ and individually members of it.

1 Corinthians 12:27

to be continued . . . What makes you different from everybody else in the world?

47 *Get to know people of all ages*

Once it was more common for generations of a family to live near or even with each other. Grandparents who lived under the same roof or just down the street from children and grandchildren were the norm and not the exception. The advancement of technology, the availability of transportation, and the expansion of big corporations have led to the dispersion of family members who often live so far from one another that they go for years without any face-to-face contact.

In some situations, it's probably good to have some distance between adult children and their parents. But one of the biggest drawbacks is that there is less interaction among the generations.

You can do something about this without uprooting your family and moving back to your place of birth. The church family provides lots of opportunities for generations to interact.

There are bound to be older adults in your congregation who would love to spend time with you and your children. Adopt a "grandparent" and invite that person to join you for dinner, to attend a school event, to be part of a birthday celebration. Match up your child with an older adult, and let them be pen pals. Send letters and drawings and photos back and forth. Children practice their writing skills, adults have willing listeners, and both have the joy of receiving mail. Adults who don't have young children at home anymore will love to have some "refrigerator art."

Sit with folks in church who are not in the same age group as you or your children.

Visit nursing homes or senior centers for activities or special events. Your church may organize a Christmas caroling party, which is fine, but find some opportunities for one-on-one interactions with those who live at the home year-round.

Volunteer to work with the high school youth group, especially if your kids are younger. Your children will love having all those "big brothers and sisters," and it's great for the teens to have younger kids around who *aren't* their little brothers and sisters. You'll be less fearful about your own children heading into their teen years if you have positive interactions with teens and find out how wonderful, fun, creative, and spiritual they are.

Go to high school events, such as plays and sporting events.

Interview an older adult at church. Use a tape recorder or video camera or take notes. Ask a variety of questions: Where were you born? What was your favorite subject in school? What was your first job? Did your family have special Christmas traditions? Who was the president when you voted for the first time? Make a little scrapbook or DVD and give a copy to the adult you interviewed.

If you're fortunate enough to live near older relatives, don't limit your intergenerational contacts to family members only. Get to know their friends, too.

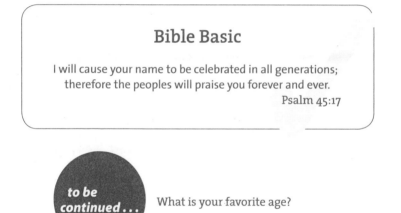

Bible Basic

I will cause your name to be celebrated in all generations; therefore the peoples will praise you forever and ever.

Psalm 45:17

to be continued . . .   What is your favorite age?

48 *Practice hospitality*

In the marriage service often used by the Presbyterian Church (U.S.A.), the prayer offered after the wedding vows and rings have been exchanged includes the lines, "Fill them with such love and joy that they may build a home of peace and welcome." To have a home where others are welcome is a godly gift, a spiritual practice in the truest sense of the word.

According to clergywoman and author Nanette Sawyer, three qualities are inherent in spiritual hospitality: receptivity, reverence, and generosity.[19] Receptivity comes from within, as we prepare ourselves to graciously receive others into our lives. Reverence is the way we honor and welcome others into our presence. Generosity reflects our ability to offer physical, emotional, and spiritual care. Spiritual hospitality, according to Sawyer, transforms us as well as those whom we bless with this gift. Hospitality is an attitude more than an action.

You don't have to have a fancy home or be an expert cook or entertainer to extend hospitality. Hospitality is not about entertainment, although that is often how it is understood. Remember a time when you needed a friend and someone took the time to listen to you, without judgment, so that when you went forward with your day you did so with newfound peace and calm. You experienced hospitality.

There are plenty of ways your family can actively practice hospitality. Sawyer suggests "awareness, acceptance, and action"[20] as a guideline for extending hospitality. Notice what's going on in the world around you so that you recognize opportunities for showing hospitality. Keep an eye out for visitors at church. Introduce yourself and sit with them. Offer to help newcomers find their way around the church or neighborhood.

Welcome new neighbors. Cut some flowers from your garden or share a plate of cookies (homemade or store-bought, it doesn't really matter). Offer to help unload the moving van, or invite their children over to play so that the parents can unpack boxes. Make a map of the local grocery stores, banks, libraries, and schools.

Be an attentive listener. Offer unhurried time and attention to your own family as well as friends and strangers. Practice hospitality with the people you love most, not just those you see only on occasion.

Hospitality is not something you offer with the expectation that the other person must return the favor. If you welcome someone into your home and convey the sense that "you owe me," hospitality is replaced by obligation, and that diminishes the gift.

Practice hospitality by cultivating a home where others feel at home. Cultivate a heart that welcomes people into your life, whether for a lifetime or for a moment. Build a home and a life where people find peace and welcome, and you will find it, too.

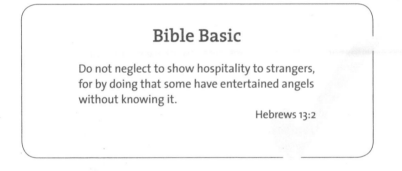

Bible Basic

Do not neglect to show hospitality to strangers, for by doing that some have entertained angels without knowing it.

Hebrews 13:2

to be continued ...

Whom would you identify as a person who conveys gracious hospitality?

49 *Share chores*

Chores are the ongoing responsibilities that nobody wants to do. The word "chores" even sounds boring and dull.

Such is the nature of chores, however; they have to get done, and somebody has to do them, like it or not. The other thing about chores: they have to be done over and over again, world without end.

For young children, chores can actually be fun. Toddlers often proclaim, "I want to help!" or "Can I try that?" That's the time to get your child involved in doing chores.

Start young and start simple. As soon as a child is able to dress himself, he's old enough to learn to put dirty laundry in a hamper or sort clean socks. As a child grows, chores can be increased, along with the skill necessary to do them.

Make it a game. Can you match the socks into pairs? Good for you! Now, can you put the matching pairs into your drawer? You're doing a great job!

Avoid the temptation to redo your child's work. So what if the bedspread isn't as straight as you would like? If the child has made her best effort, let it be. Redoing the work only leaves the child feeling inadequate and adds to your workload.

Let your children figure out their own way to do things. Your way is not the only way, nor always the best. Give your children the tools they need, teach them how they are used, and let them figure out the rest. Maybe you like to pile up all the dirty dishes before you begin to rinse them off, but your child would rather clear the dishes from the table one by one. What does it matter? Learn to let go of the need to be in control.

Instead of assigning chores, negotiate with your children which chores are their responsibility. The more they can help decide who does what, the more likely they are to carry out their responsibilities. Maybe they will decide to trade off chores with a sibling. If it works for both of them, that's fine. Creative negotiating can be a good skill to learn.

Common mistakes: We take on all the chores, because it's easier than trying to ride herd on a bunch of reluctant kids. Or we start doing all the chores as the kids get older and busier with school and activities. Those solutions are all right now and then, but they don't teach our children how to balance their lives so that they can do the things they need to do along with the things they want to do.

Children learn self-esteem by being given responsibilities and being held accountable. Our stress level is decreased when we have a little help. Both are worthy reasons to assign a few chores.

And while you're at it, why not come up with a better name than "chores"? How about "privileges"?

Bible Basic

As we work together with him, we urge you also not to accept the grace of God in vain.

2 Corinthians 6:1

to be continued . . . What chore was your responsibility as you were growing up?

50 Discuss what you've learned at church

Families have such busy schedules, we rarely get to digest what we've just experienced because we're in a hurry to check one thing off the calendar before we race off to the next event. Basketball practice? Check! Curriculum night at school? Check! Music lessons and dinner and homework and youth group? *CheckCheckCheckCheck!*

Church becomes confined to an hour on Sunday morning, another component in an activity-packed week, come and gone without any time to even think about what happened.

Sunday school? Worship? Check and check!

It's good to take time to think about your weekly activities, not simply to rush through them. This goes for church, too.

Rehashing your morning at church doesn't have to be a formal event. Ask questions on the way home or while you're having lunch. Sprinkle questions throughout the week, especially as they are triggered by other circumstances. When your child comes home from school upset about a fight on the playground, tie it into what you learned at church, as long as it isn't forced. "Remember how we heard the story of Joseph and his brothers this past week? Do you think there could have been some jealousy involved in that fight?"

Having an open discussion about what was said in worship lets your child know that you value his opinion and that she has a right to think about issues of faith for herself. One need not always agree with what the preacher says. You can be blunt about this: "Did you agree with what the pastor said?" or "What do you think you would have said if you had preached the sermon today?"

Sermons are only part of a church and worship experience, of course. Ask your child, "What was your favorite part of worship today? Did you enjoy the music? What prayers do you remember? OK, so you were bored. Why is that? What might have kept your interest?"

Find out what lessons and stories are being taught in Sunday school. Share with your child what you're studying, too. It's a nice reminder that learning about our faith doesn't stop when we graduate from high school, but is a lifelong—and exciting—endeavor.

At supper one night, reread the Scripture heard in worship that week. When possible, find out what the Scripture readings are going to be the following week and look over them with your child ahead of time, so you both feel prepared.

It's not just the facts but the interactions that happen among the people that enrich our church experience: how your child's Sunday school teacher handled a disagreement in class; the response of the congregation when the prayer requests were mentioned; the laughter during the children's time when that little boy yelled, "Hi, Mom!" Reliving these interactions may be the most important learning that takes place all week.

Bible Basic

From the rising of the sun to its setting
the name of the Lord is to be praised.

Psalm 113:3

What did you enjoy most about your time at church this week?

51 *Express physical affection*

There is no greater feeling in the world than your baby, peaceful and warm, snuggled on your shoulder, nestled in your neck.

That's a parent's point of view. By all appearances, the baby feels the same way.

Physical affection is necessary for the healthy development of a child. Infants deprived of physical nurture and comfort develop emotional and cognitive difficulties as they grow. Hugs, kisses, and snuggles, with people who would never even think about abusing this in any way, help children grow into healthy, loving adults.

Children should see their parents being affectionate with one another, within limits of course. Hold hands when you're out for a walk or sitting next to each other on the couch. It's all right to hug and kiss your husband or wife in front of the kids. You don't have to go overboard. But if a child sees adults lovingly offer and receive physical affection, it will seem like the natural way to be.

Do not force your child into physical displays of affection. People think it's cute to guilt their little ones into giving kisses and hugs: "Your uncle is going to be sad forever if you don't give him a kiss!" Avoid that kind of motivation. Instead, say something that provides your child with a choice, such as, "If you would like to give your uncle a hug, I'll bet that will make him smile! But if you don't want to give a hug, I know he'll smile for you anyhow." Give the child the option. Respect the child's boundaries. A child who learns that it is acceptable to say no when young will be more at ease saying no when she is a teenager and being pressured into a situation that might not be in her best interest.

Some families hug each other every time they say hello or good-bye. If this is the way your family works, there's nothing wrong with it. If your family chooses to be a little less affectionate, that's OK, too. Every family has to discover what works best for them.

Many parents wonder at what age a child should no longer be allowed to crawl into bed with them for a snuggle. As long as the child chooses to do this without any prompting by the parent, it is probably fine. Children seem to have an innate sense about when it's time to stop. Not many high schoolers want to climb into bed with their mom or dad before catching the bus in the morning. Chances are, your kids will be ready to give up the snuggle routine long before you are. Cherish the time while you can.

Physical affection is one of the most wonderful blessings a family can share with one another. Children may outgrow the need for a security blanket, but never the security of growing up within an affectionate, loving family.

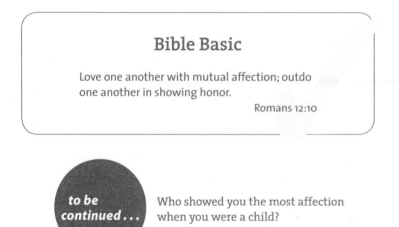

Bible Basic

Love one another with mutual affection; outdo one another in showing honor.

Romans 12:10

to be continued . . . Who showed you the most affection when you were a child?

52 *Choose a family song*

We connect to one another through music. The importance of having music in your home is highlighted elsewhere in this book (see entry 75), but you can also choose a family song that you can sing whenever the mood strikes and whenever your moods need lifted.

Pick a song that says something about your family. The popular song by the group Sister Sledge from the late 1970s, "We Are Family," not only has a great title and a catchy beat, but the lyrics are fitting, too: "We are family, everybody get up and sing!"[21]

"Ninety-nine bottles of beer on the wall," on the other hand . . .

Sometimes, a song seems to choose you. When you rock your little boy to sleep one night, you find yourself singing "All through the Night," and after that, it's the song you sing to him every night. Long after those nighttime lullabies end, you both get a special feeling whenever that hymn is sung in church.

Pick an old favorite or write your own lyrics to a familiar tune. Write your own music if you feel so inspired, with original words or words of a favorite poem.

Once your family has picked (or written) a favorite song, there are multiple ways to enjoy it.

- Sing the song for grace or as the end of a prayer at night.
- Whistle or hum a few bars of the song when you're in a crowd. People will think it's a random tune, but your family will know better and get a kick out of being in on the secret that belongs to them alone.
- Soothe an ill child's sick and weary spirit with the words and music of the family song.
- Play the song on your CD player and dance. Invite visitors to dance to the song with you. Teach them the words and sing at the top of your lungs.
- Create a Christmas present by adding a recording of the song to a DVD slide show of family photos.

Songs are portable; you carry them in your head and in your heart. You can access the song at any time, with just a little effort on the part of your vocal cords.

Bible Basic

O sing to the Lord a new song;
sing to the Lord, all the earth.

Psalm 96:1

What song title describes your family?

53 *Tackle the tough topics*

Some topics make parents want to become like ostriches and bury their heads in the sand. If only we could block out the world and avoid dealing with tough topics like sex, drugs, and alcohol. But we are not ostriches, and it is up to us as parents to talk about anything and everything with our children, even if it makes us uncomfortable.

There is no foolproof equation that can guarantee our child's safe passage through life. Love + education + awareness of the facts does not always equal good decisions. You can talk to your child about the implications of having sex, the risks of using drugs, and the consequences of alcohol abuse, but this might not keep your child from experimenting with any and all of these. Still, your child needs to be able to talk with you about all these issues and more, in an atmosphere that allows both of you to speak your views and be heard.

Think through your own feelings on these topics. If you grew up in a family with an alcoholic parent, you know firsthand the implications of alcohol abuse, which makes this an especially volatile issue for you. Your overriding need to protect your child from alcohol may make it difficult for you to handle it when she comes home from a friend's house smelling of beer. By taking time to talk with your spouse, other parents, and even a counselor (if the topic is especially emotional for you) before you need to have these conversations with your child, you will foster an atmosphere that allows your child to form his or her own opinions. On the other hand, it's not wrong for your child to understand your position and to recognize that you have valid reasons for feeling the way that you do.

You may be tempted to use guilt to keep your child from experimenting with situations that have the potential to be dangerous. Don't. Guilt is not a constructive emotion. Guilt may lead your child to skirt the truth or keep secrets. Just as unhealthy, guilt may cause your child to harbor negative feelings about sexuality, for instance, and sexuality and sex are complicated enough without adding guilt and shame to the equation.

Use teachable moments as prompts to talk about important issues. A story on the news, an event that happens in your community, even a sermon that invites reflection on a lifestyle choice can be a springboard into a conversation with your child. A magazine article on teen pregnancy can segue into a conversation on birth control, abortion, adoption. You probably have strong opinions, but reserve judgment. Like guilt, judgment of other people's choices isn't necessary or helpful.

If you wait until your child is in her teens before trying to foster open communication, it may be too late. The earlier in life your child knows that she can talk to you about anything, the better off you'll both be when she has questions or is faced with a situation where your support and guidance are needed. Still, it's better late than never.

It takes a lot of time and energy to walk with your child through the many issues that he will—and must—face on the road to maturity. Remember to nurture your own spirit as you travel on this journey of parenthood.

Bible Basic

This is God,
our God forever and ever.
He will be our guide forever.
Psalm 48:14

to be continued . . .

Did you grow up in a home where tough topics were dealt with openly?

54 *Read aloud*

At the end of a long day, Daddy rocks his three-year-old and reads aloud from her favorite book. The little girl knows the story by heart. Daddy reads it to her every night, sometimes more than once. She nestles in her Daddy's arms, and the steady sound of his voice soothes and comforts her. Daddy breathes in the sweet perfume of baby shampoo, and when his child drifts off to sleep, he closes the book and continues to rock her, humming softly. All seems right with the world.

This is a God-moment. As parent and child focus only on each other, the world slows down and the chaos is pushed aside. Loving bonds are deepened, and the sense of peace and trust experienced in the short time it takes to read one book replicates the loving relationship that God has for us.

Fill your home with books. Make a weekly outing to the library and bring home stacks of books. Many bookstores welcome people to browse without having to make a purchase. There are entire sections just for children, with tables and chairs and floor pillows that welcome readers to sit and leaf through a pile of books.

Read *to* and *with* your children. Children who see their parents reading on a regular basis learn that reading isn't just for kids. A family reading night is an alternative to the constant barrage of TV shows.

When you read and reread a favorite book to your child, the flow of the story and the particular words become integrated in the child's heart and mind. Pause as you are reading, and let your child fill in the missing word. Books with rhyming text allow a child to catch on quickly, to guess the word that is going to rhyme, and to remember it the next time you read the book.

If your children are of an age to read, let them read aloud to you. You can take turns reading aloud to each other. Be patient when your child sounds out an unfamiliar word. Take a moment to explain the meaning of a word that your child doesn't understand.

Read a book of Bible stories and assign each member of the family a different part in the story. Do a "read through," practicing the parts and getting a feel for the voices and intonation that express each character. You can carry this to the next level and add costumes or props and turn the story into a theatrical play, even if the only audience is the other members of the family.

Audiobooks are another good way to hear stories read aloud, sometimes in the voice of the author. Audiobooks are great to have on car trips, but you can gather around and listen to them in your living room, too.

Long before the Bible was written down and consolidated into the biblical text we use today, the stories were passed along using the oral tradition. The stories of faith were told aloud, and often, to generations of the faithful. We claim this essential part of our faith tradition when we continue to read aloud, to tell the old, old stories to our children, and to make these stories come alive within the hearts of the next generation.

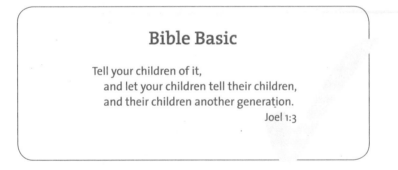

Bible Basic

Tell your children of it,
    and let your children tell their children,
    and their children another generation.

Joel 1:3

to be continued . . .   What is your favorite children's book?

55 *Have a secret signal*

Athletes do it all the time.

The running back scores a touchdown, falls to his knees, and folds his hands in prayer. The all-star basketball player shoots a three-pointer and holds up her index finger—"I'm number one!" The outfielder hits a grand slam, and as he rounds the bases, he thumps his chest with his fist and points to the crowd, with the obvious message, "I love you guys!"

Signals are used in many walks of life. The traffic cop blows his whistle and points to where the cars should turn. Auctioneers pay keen attention to the slight hand motions of the crowd, indicating a bid. The parent sitting in church waves frantically at her child standing in front of the church singing with his finger halfway up his nose.

Devise a secret signal to use with your child. If you have more than one child, you should have a different secret signal for each. The secret signal should be simple and subtle, because this is only between the two of you. A tug of the ear, a hand on the heart, or a nod of the head; any of these will do. Come up with something that honors a special connection you have with your child. For instance, if you and your child enjoy singing together, your secret signal could be the touch of your two fingers on your lips. Once the secret signal is sent, the other person responds with the same secret signal. You've made a connection!

American Sign Language has some wonderful signs that you can use or incorporate into your secret signal. When making the sign for "joy," place your hand, palm toward you, on your chest, and brush upward two times. This secret signal is a way of saying, "you bring me joy." Check online for other ideas using ASL.

Use the secret signal to make contact from a distance, when you're too far away to say something without being overheard. Use the secret signal just for the fun of it, as you tuck your child into bed at night. Use the secret signal any time you want to make a quick connection with your child.

When your daughter strides to the front of the school auditorium to make her first public speech and glances quickly over to where you're sitting, a flash of the secret signal brings her a bit of reassurance.

When your son heads off to summer camp for two weeks, his face pressed against the window of the bus as it rolls down the road, a flash of the secret signal makes the parting a bit more bearable.

When that same son grows up and heads off to college, and you're standing in tears watching him pass through security at the airport, and he turns and makes the secret signal, you know that this simple gesture that you've had for all these years, just the two of you, is a bond that lasts a lifetime.

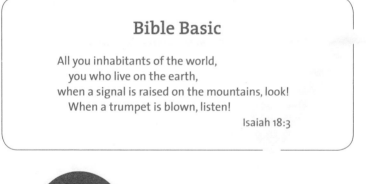

Bible Basic

All you inhabitants of the world,
    you who live on the earth,
when a signal is raised on the mountains, look!
    When a trumpet is blown, listen!

Isaiah 18:3

to be continued . . .

What are some ways you can use a secret signal to connect with your child?

56 *Create a safe retreat*

The world is a scary place. Even a child who is too young to read the newspaper or to be aware of crime and natural disasters can experience the world as a frightening place. The kindly woman in the checkout line at the grocery store who makes an exaggerated face and says in a loud voice, "Oh, now *where* did you get those *curls*?" may not mean to frighten a shy toddler, but that may be the result.

As a child begins to experience the anxiety of separation from the parent, fears crop up: fears of the unknown, of strangers, of the cruel way people treat one another. These fears make it all the more important that a child is able to find refuge and safety in the home. The stresses and strains in any family also make it necessary to create a place to retreat to within your own environs.

You can declare one room or corner of a room to be a conflict-free zone. No harsh words, arguments, or negative thoughts are allowed when the family, or individual family member, is in this room. If a child has had a particularly rough day, finding safety and calm in that one room can ease the tensions and soothe the spirit and make it easier to regroup and face the world again the next day.

One family dubs their large bed the Boat. When family members need a place to withdraw from the world, regroup, and find refuge together, they make a voyage on the Boat. Stuffed toys, games, CDs, and even a few snacks are gathered, and everyone climbs into the Boat for a few hours of "smooth sailing." While on the Boat, they are out at sea, away from troubling people and problems that are not allowed to follow them. When everyone in the family is relaxed and has had a chance to put some distance between themselves and their worries, the Boat "sails" back to land and the family disembarks, feeling grounded once more.

Whatever space you designate, make it sacred ground. Nobody and nothing is allowed to disrupt the peace and calm of this place. Feel free, as a parent, to escape to this stress-free island now and then. Author Joyce Rupp writes, "When we close the door to external activity, we pause to be in solidarity with the One who enriches and restores our inner balance. We give ourselves to silent communion with our divine guide who leads us to the richness of our authentic self and encourages us to share this goodness with others."[22] Give yourself a time-out, and bask in the peace of Christ's presence. It's good for the soul.

If you have a safe place where you can find peace when you are feeling overwhelmed, you will be more able to be a calming presence when your child needs a refuge from the storms and chaos of everyday life.

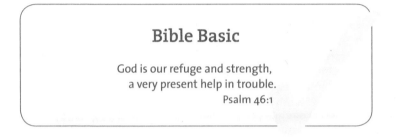

Bible Basic

God is our refuge and strength,
a very present help in trouble.
Psalm 46:1

to be continued . . .

Where was your place of safety when you were a child?

57 *Turn off the TV*

. . . and the cell phone (and the landline if you still have one) and the computer and the gaming system and any other kind of electronic device that demands your family's time and attention. These devices take up more time every day.

Children spend more and more time with electronic media, and parents know less and less about what their children are doing. Gone are the days when friends called the house and parents answered the phone and knew at least the names of those with whom their children interacted.

From 2004 to 2009, the average amount of time that children ages eight to eighteen spent with electronic media increased by nearly one and a half hours per day. Young people spend an average of seven hours and thirty-eight minutes *daily* in these pursuits. That's fifty-three hours a week, more than a full-time job. That doesn't even include multitasking, which increases the numbers.[23]

When parents set a few limits, the amount of time children spend on electronic media decreases significantly and school grades improve. Limit the number of text messages that can be sent and received, and block them altogether during certain hours. Share a family computer instead of using personal laptops in separate rooms.

What kind of example are you setting for your child? Do you have TVs in every room? Do you turn on the computer and the TV as soon as you walk in the door? Are you constantly in front of your laptop, checking e-mail or surfing the Web? Do you answer your cell phone every time it rings, even when you know the call can wait? Count the hours you spend each day and you may be surprised. Kids aren't the only ones who spend too much time with modern media.

Read instead of watching TV. Turn off cell phones during meals. Leave the computer off for an evening. When you're in the car, leave the radio off and talk, or play some of those silly games families used to play on car trips before everyone had a set of headphones and traveling TV.

We can be accessed every minute of every day by people in all parts of the world. This does have its benefits, but we need to be aware of the drawbacks and protect our family time and our children. There's something to be said for taking a step back from constant accessibility and bombardment of the senses. Tune out the TV and tune into God, who has always been able to be reached anytime, from anywhere, long before Facebook and text messages.

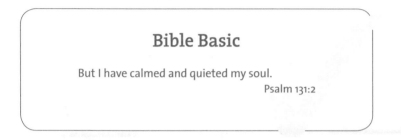

Bible Basic

But I have calmed and quieted my soul.

Psalm 131:2

to be continued ...

If you had to give up your cell phone, how would that change your life?

58 *Cook meals together*

If we added up the time we spend shopping for groceries, cooking meals, washing dishes, and cleaning up the kitchen, we would either realize how essential cooking and eating are or we would sit down and cry at how much time it all takes. We can't live without eating, and it does take up a lot of time, so families might as well use meal preparation as an opportunity to spend time together.

Most newspapers have weekly sections on food trends and advertisements for sales at grocery stores. You can use this as a starting point for meal planning. Kids can help clip coupons and make lists. Flip through cookbooks and recipe cards and choose a few recipes that you all agree sound tasty. Then find a day on the calendar—perhaps the same day each week—and mark it as the family cook fest.

Once you've put together a list of ingredients, check your cupboards to see what you have and what you need. Take your kids with you to the grocery store so that they can learn how to choose items and compare prices. Whenever possible, shop at a local farmers market. Grow a few of your own vegetables or herbs. In this way, children learn good stewardship of the earth's resources and come to appreciate the fact that other people work to grow and produce the food that we often take for granted.

Use simple cookbooks that everyone can follow. Gather your supplies and divide up the tasks. Everyone has to work as a team.

As kids help with preparing a meal, they learn skills that will be valuable all their lives. Learning how to measure ingredients is an obvious lesson, but there's more to cooking together than simple math. As everyone helps, children also learn that their contribution is valued by the whole family, even if they do spill more flour than they get in the bowl.

Get creative! Invent a new recipe. Make your own version of stone soup where everyone chooses one ingredient and you cook them together—with some guidelines, of course. The ingredients must be edible and items that everyone in the family can eat.

Make extra portions to freeze as leftovers for busy days. Pack up a meal and take it to a friend recovering from an illness or someone who lives alone.

Keep a journal of which recipes work and which ones don't. Jot notes in the cookbook or on recipe cards.

Create your own family cookbook. Internet resources can help you create a cookbook with photos and stories, but you can do this on your own, too. It makes a great gift for the extended family and a priceless keepsake of your own.

Planning and cooking a meal together as a family may take time, but it is time well spent and a recipe for success.

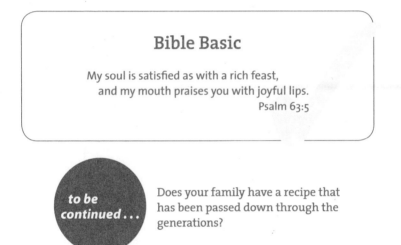

Bible Basic

My soul is satisfied as with a rich feast,
and my mouth praises you with joyful lips.
Psalm 63:5

to be continued . . .

Does your family have a recipe that has been passed down through the generations?

59 *Be still*

Taking time to be still isn't quite the same as closing your eyes for a quick nap, although that can be part of it. Being still is a spiritual practice that soothes your soul, connects you to God, and sometimes makes it possible for you to endure a stressful time.

Plenty of times you tell your child, "Please be quiet!" or "Please sit still!" Imagine God saying the same thing to you when you are filling your prayers with petitions or running around in circles getting nothing done.

Be still. Be intentional about being still.

Make it manageable: five minutes of stillness on any given day. Five minutes is barely enough, but it will do.

Find a quiet place. If that is impossible, find a place where you can at least close your eyes and block out the noise around you.

Get in a rhythm of breathing. Breathe slowly in, through your nose; breathe slowly out, through your mouth. Breathe slowly in, breathe slowly out. Expand your lungs by breathing deeply, expanding your abdomen as you breathe in, tightening it a bit as you breathe out. Be aware of your breath. Let it fill you with much-needed oxygen; then let it dispel the carbon dioxide. Breathe in calm; breathe out stress.

Listen to the sounds around you. If you are in a quiet place, you might be surprised by all the sounds that surround you, sounds you might not have noticed in the noisiness of everyday life. The hum of the lightbulbs. The deep blast of a foghorn in the distance. The soft rattle of leaves as a breeze blows past. Listen to the sounds, but do not let them distract you.

Breathe, and listen. That's all you have to do.

You can pray if you wish. Nothing wordy or extensive, mind you; just a word or two. "Thank you" will do. Or "God, help me." Pray a word that reflects how you feel or what you long for: "Love." "Peace." "Strength."

Let your children know that you take this time to be still. Be still in front of them, every now and then. Let them try it, too. Being still is a spiritual practice that we all need to do, and the sooner we learn this the better.

When Jesus learned that John the Baptist had been beheaded, he "withdrew from there in a boat to a deserted place by himself" (Matthew 14:13). Jesus needed some quiet time, alone time, time with God, to grieve the loss of his cousin and friend, the one who had paved the way for his entrance into public ministry. Only after Jesus took this time was he able to minister to the multitudes that followed him and gathered on the shore, awaiting his return.

Just as our bodies need restful sleep in order to heal and rebuild, our spirits need rest to heal from the hurts of life, to regain energy and joy.

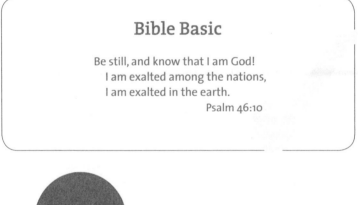

Bible Basic

Be still, and know that I am God!
I am exalted among the nations,
I am exalted in the earth.
Psalm 46:10

to be continued . . .

What sounds do you hear that you didn't notice before?

60 *Ask the right questions*

You wait for your child to arrive home from a day at school. Your intentions are good—you want to be a good listener, to hear about your child's day, to talk about any issues that arose during the day. A plate of cookies and a glass of milk are on the table, a surefire way to start a loving heart-to-heart talk.

Your child bangs through the door and drops his backpack on the floor. "Hi, honey!" you greet him cheerily. "How was your day?"

"Fine," he says as he grabs a cookie and heads out the door to play.

Is that all you're going to get, after all your preparation? A one-word answer? Some days, you're lucky to get that much!

There's a fine art to asking questions that encourage at least a brief response. "How was your day?" is not one of them.

When you ask your child a question, narrow your focus. Instead of the usual "How was your day?" try asking, "What made you happiest in school today?"

The setting is important, too. Some children may not want to sit face to face and talk at the kitchen table, but once you're in the car driving to soccer practice, the words flow. Be ready with listening ears when they do talk!

Your child may not be ready to talk when you are. After a busy day at school, she might need a little time to herself. Make yourself available, and let your child know that you will listen whenever she has something to share. The more interactions you have with your child during the day, the more opportunities you'll have to engage in conversations with your child. Fixing a meal together, going for a walk, reading books in the evening (without the TV!), and playing a game all provide opportunities for you and your child to talk. Spend time with your child; enter into his world. This can be life changing—for you.

Nobel Peace Prize winner and author Elie Wiesel wrote that when his mother greeted him after a day at school, she would not ask, "What did you do today?" or "What did you learn?" or "To whom did you speak?" Her question was always the same: "Did you have a good question today?"[24] Beyond eliciting a yes or a no, a question like that prompts some thoughtful reflection that provides an opportunity not only for conversation but also for plumbing the depths of those inner conversations that are going on within us.

Bible Basic

To make an apt answer is a joy to anyone,
and a word in season, how good it is!
Proverbs 15:23

to be continued . . .

What is the best question you've ever been asked?

61 Be honest

Let's be honest: everybody lies.

"How do you like my new haircut?" a wife asks her husband. "I love it!" he responds, but he's thinking, "How could she have cut her hair so short? It looks awful!"

"I feel great!" you tell your best friend, even though your head is pounding, because you know she really wants to go see that new movie with you.

"Did you take the dog out this afternoon?" "I did!" your child responds, instead of admitting that he forgot, and only later do you find the mess that the dog left in the corner.

We tell little white lies because we know that sometimes the truth hurts. Or it just seems easier than saying how we really feel. Or we're afraid of consequences. We tell little white lies for a lot of reasons, but none of those reasons are worth the price of being dishonest.

Albert Einstein said, "Whoever is careless with the truth in small matters cannot be trusted with important matters."[25] Being complacent about telling little lies makes it easier to tell bigger ones. Every time we tell a lie, we pave the road for another one. The more lies told, the more difficult it becomes to get back to the truth, because we build a phony structure that depends on lies to keep it standing.

Don't tell lies because they're convenient, even if they seem slight, and never ask your child to tell a lie on your behalf. When the phone rings and your child answers it because you don't want to be interrupted, have him tell the truth: "My dad can't come to the phone right now," instead of "My dad isn't home."

If you catch your child about to tell a lie, give her another chance. "Are you sure you don't know how that toy got broken? Telling the truth is more important than breaking a toy. Maybe you want to answer that question again." Affirm when your child tells the truth, and make a big deal about it. "I'm proud of you for telling the truth. Good for you!"

Share with your child situations you encounter in which telling the truth was difficult, but you did it anyway, and you're proud of yourself. "My boss thought I wrote the report that got such a good review, but it was really my coworker. I spoke up and told the truth, even though that meant that I didn't get the bonus. I'm glad I did the right thing, because I wouldn't have felt right if I got the credit when I didn't deserve it."

If telling the truth means your child has to admit to a wrongdoing, make the praise for telling the truth greater than the discipline for what the child did wrong. "Because you told the truth about taking the money that didn't belong to you, I am going to let you go to the birthday party. However, because you did take something that wasn't yours, you are not going to be able to stay overnight."

Be honest. Tell the truth. Your child deserves no less. Honesty really is the best policy, every time.

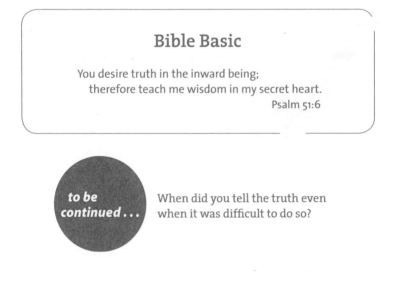

Bible Basic

You desire truth in the inward being;
therefore teach me wisdom in my secret heart.
Psalm 51:6

to be continued . . . When did you tell the truth even when it was difficult to do so?

62 *Fill in your family faith tree*

A family faith tree is similar to a family tree, but the family's faith journey is its main focus. You may be surprised what you discover about your faith heritage once you start trying to fill in the branches of this tree.

To start off, think about the faith traditions with which you were raised. Did your family attend church? What are your earliest memories of worship and Sunday school? What holidays did you celebrate and how? Who were the family members who taught you about faith? Were you baptized? When and where? Write down everything, even if you don't use it all.

Grandparents, aunts, uncles, and cousins may answer some of these questions for you. If someone serves as the family genealogist, find out what you can about your family history. You might be surprised to discover that your great-great-uncle was a circuit-riding preacher in the old West or that your grandmother changed from one denomination to another when she came to this country to start a new life far from her roots.

Perhaps you don't come from a churchgoing family and don't know where to begin creating a family faith tree. If you don't know anything about the faith of your ancestors, don't let that stop you from creating a family faith tree with your children. Start with your immediate family. Your children can carry on the tradition and fill in the branches as they grow up and have families of their own.

Once you have some information, sketch a tree on a sheet of paper or download a graphic from a Web site devoted to family tree research. Write "God" on the trunk of the tree. We are God's children, after all, so we belong on God's family tree and God belongs on ours.

Write your name, and the names of your children, on leaves that you add to the branches on the tree. Along with the name, fill in the faith history you know: baptism dates, denominational affiliations, and so on. Leave room to write in more information as you discover it. Add leaves to the tree as children are born or adopted into the family.

Cut out some fruit shapes: apples or oranges or pears or pineapples. On each of these fruits, write down the attributes of faith that are important to your family. Use Galatians 5:22–23 for ideas: "The fruit of the Spirit is love, joy, peace, patience, kindness, generosity, faithfulness, gentleness, and self-control." Add others: grace, forgiveness, joy, gratitude. Place these "fruits of the Spirit" in the branches of your tree.

Even if you can't track down much about your particular family's faith traditions, you have a faith history, because our faith roots go back to the beginning of time.

Bible Basic

By contrast, the fruit of the Spirit is love, joy, peace, patience, kindness, generosity, faithfulness, gentleness, and self-control.

Galatians 5:22–23

to be continued . . .

As you investigate your family faith tree, what have you learned about your ancestors?

63 *Read the Bible together*

Not long ago Bibles were available in only a few translations, and none were written in language that young children could understand.

Now there are more Bibles to choose from than anyone could read. Even so-called children's Bibles flood the bookshelves, with new ones being published every season.

Too many options can be overwhelming, but one thing is for sure: there's a Bible for every person, every age. Narrowing your selection is the biggest challenge. If you need help, ask your pastor for suggestions or go to the bookstore and browse. Take your child along, if she is old enough, and let her help you choose a Bible that you can read together.

Reading the Bible with your child should start long before your child can write letters, let alone read. You do the reading to begin with, and as the years pass your child can start reading to you. Take turns reading to one another.

Children need stories that are the right length for their attention span. For a young child just starting to learn the Bible, choose a Bible storybook that focuses on the beloved stories. Bible picture books offer colorful artwork that holds a child's attention as you read aloud. Make sure that you pause and look at the pictures, too.

Don't rush. If your child asks a question, pause for a moment—the story will wait. Engage your child in the answer. "Why is the rainbow in the sky? Maybe because that's a good place for lots of people to see it. What do you think?" A very young child might not be ready to hear the details about light passing through moisture in the atmosphere, although there will come a time for that kind of information. The loving time you spend snuggled next to your child, reading the stories of God over and over, matters more than trying to plow through a certain number of pages each night.

If your child is old enough to attend a church school class, find out what Bible stories are being taught and reread these stories at home. This reinforces the learning of the story and increases the connection between what the child learns at church and what he learns at home.

You may still have a Bible that you read when you were growing up. Show it to your child and share the stories you remember about when you received the Bible, who read it to you, and which stories were your favorites.

Many Bibles have a concordance in the back, a section that lists words and the verses where those words are found. Have a treasure hunt, choosing words and finding them in the Bible. Take time to explore the maps, illustrations, and other supplementary material that your Bible contains.

Remember that old church school song "The B-I-B-L-E, yes that's the book for me!" Let the Bible be the book for you, and for your family, too.

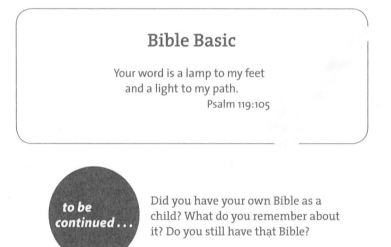

Bible Basic

Your word is a lamp to my feet
and a light to my path.
Psalm 119:105

to be continued . . .

Did you have your own Bible as a child? What do you remember about it? Do you still have that Bible?

64 *Say thank you*

The great Christian mystic Meister Eckhart wrote, "If the only prayer you ever said was thank you, that would be enough."

Who among us ever gets tired of being told thank you? Those two little words are a wonderful affirmation that we are appreciated not just for what we do but for who we are.

Saying thank you begins at home. Say thank you to your husband or wife, your parents, your children.

Don't wait for some grand gesture or gift before you say thanks. Say thank you for the little things. "Thank you for setting the table. Thank you for holding the door for me. Thank you for feeding the dog. Thank you for playing with your little sister." Kids thrive on being told thank you. The more they hear it, the more they'll learn to say it, too.

Say thanks to the people who serve you: the mail carrier, the person who bags your groceries, the waiter who keeps refilling your water glass and who cleans up the mess you're bound to leave at a restaurant when you dine out with children. It may be the person's job to serve you, but thank that person nonetheless. There are a lot of thankless jobs in the world and plenty of people who take advantage of those whose job it is to serve them in one way or another. You could make someone's day brighter by your words of gratitude, and you set a good example for your children.

Say thank you to those who give you gifts, even family members. Teach your children the importance of writing thank-you notes or making a phone call when they receive a gift. Grandmas and grandpas appreciate being thanked, even though they probably would buy the gifts anyway just because they love their grandchildren.

Your words of thanks should be sincere. You may not like the color of the sweater your great-aunt sent you, but you can appreciate her thoughtfulness and the spirit in which she gave the gift.

Say thank you to God. "Thank you, God, for sunshine after a cloudy day. Thank you for the gift of my family. Thank you for loving me, no matter what."

Thank you: two little words that make a big difference.

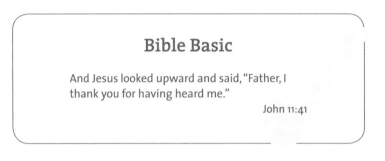

Bible Basic

And Jesus looked upward and said, "Father, I thank you for having heard me."

John 11:41

to be continued . . .

When was the last time someone thanked you?

65 *Get to know your child's friends*

Parents need to know the people their children choose as friends. This is not just about trusting or not trusting your own children or their friends. Watching your children interact with kids their own age, seeing the ways they treat one another as well as your home, and showing the friends that you are an adult who cares about them are much more important reasons to have an open-door policy.

Make your home a welcoming place, where your child's friends are comfortable hanging out. It's worth the extra mess and the strain on your grocery bill.

Children should not have friends in your home if you or another responsible adult (such as a babysitter) are not there. The rest of the rules are up to you to set and to keep. If you don't allow food to be eaten in the living room, let that be known. Set up a snack table in the kitchen, with child-friendly food and drinks. Ask the other parents about food allergies. Make sure your kids know about those allergies, so they can be alert and sensitive to their friend's needs, too.

If you're worried about the wear and tear on your furniture, throw some washable covers on the couch. Have pillows with removable covers. Or fill your house with inexpensive furniture. You don't want to be stressing out over a few spills, because they are going to happen.

Have lots of games and books around. Sponsor a game fest when all the neighborhood kids are invited to your house for board games or a day of outdoor olympics. Let your children be part of the planning. They can choose games, send invitations, make prizes. If it's raining, throw an old tablecloth on the floor and have an indoor picnic.

Stock your shelves with craft supplies: paper, crayons, cardboard, odds and ends. Items should be within reach of the kids. If there are things you don't want the kids to touch, say so or put them out of reach.

Once a month, have a movie night or a book club gathering. Use your imagination!

Invite the friends' parents over for pizza while the kids hang out. Invite them to join you for miniature golf. Invite the whole family to church, if they don't have a church home of their own.

Expect a little noise. Enjoy yourself, your children, and their friends.

If you invite your child's friends into your home, don't be shy about setting a few rules, such as "put your dishes in the sink when you're done eating" and "throw out your own trash." Let your children know that you expect them to do the same when they're at someone else's house.

Bible Basic

Welcome one another, therefore, just as Christ has welcomed you, for the glory of God.

Romans 15:7

What will you miss most when your children are grown and the house is quiet?

66 *Set boundaries*

Children need some limits. It gets more and more difficult to figure out these limits as your child grows. Setting a bedtime each school night when your child is starting kindergarten makes sense, because you know that if she doesn't get enough sleep, it's going to be difficult for her to get through the school day without a meltdown. Setting a curfew for your teenager on a school night may be greeted with an even worse temper tantrum than you got when that child was younger, but don't let that stop you. Expect some resistance. Children do need to learn to figure these things out for themselves as they grow, but they also need the security of a few boundaries.

Your child needs guidelines and parameters. Be kind, but be firm. A child who has reasonable limits feels more secure than a child who is allowed to do anything he wants to do.

Kids will try to cross the lines you set. This is part of their job as children. This is how they learn to set their own limits, which is crucial the older they get. The world is full of temptations that will continually challenge your child to make healthy or unhealthy choices. When your teenager wails, "You don't trust me!" respond, "Sure, I trust you. I trust you to be a teenager." You can relax a few rules as your child shows responsibility, but don't give in because it appears to be the easy way out. It isn't.

As your child grows, involve him in figuring out boundaries. Start when your child is young: "Would you like to have Sam over to play after school for an hour, or would you rather wait and invite him on Saturday afternoon when you don't have school and he can stay longer?" You might get the answer "Both!" but making choices is part of what helps your child learn to set his own boundaries.

Setting boundaries involves a lot more than enforcing rules and limitations. A parent also needs to protect a child from situations that become overwhelming and from people who cross boundaries without any hesitation or concern for the rights of others.

A curious child wants to try all kinds of activities. This is fine to a degree, but it's easy for children to become overloaded with too many interests. Limit the number of outside activities a child can take on at any one time. Kids get burnt out trying to do everything. Make sure your child's schedule allows free time, playtime, unscheduled time. Work that into your own life as best as you can, too.

Protect your child from "toxic" people, who think only of themselves and their own gain. They take advantage of the kindness of others. Toxic people monopolize situations and relationships to the detriment of everyone involved. A toxic person could be the "friend" who always has to have his way, who expects your child to give up her own interests and only do what the friend wants to do. If you see this happening, talk with your child. Let her know that she does not always have to give up what she wants to do because that is what a good friend does. A good friend does not expect to get his way all the time. A good friend wants to be involved in the interests of other people, especially friends.

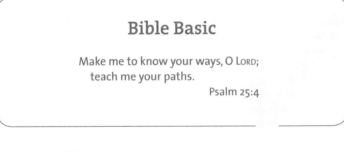

Bible Basic

Make me to know your ways, O LORD;
     teach me your paths.

Psalm 25:4

to be continued ...

What boundaries are most difficult for you to set?

67 *Celebrate for no reason*

Or celebrate for lots of reasons! Why limit celebrations to birthdays and holidays? Life should be a party, as often as possible.

Brighten up a cold winter day with festive balloons.

Have an unbirthday party. Skip the gifts and put candles on the meatloaf. Have cake, and toss in a few party favors. Keep it simple; the fun is in the surprise of it, and you'll enjoy planning and pulling off that surprise.

Throw a surprise party for a person from church who doesn't have family nearby. There are undoubtedly folks who live alone and would love to be remembered, and celebrated, by the people from their church family.

Celebrate efforts and not just accomplishments. When your child places last at the gymnastics meet, congratulate the effort. Some kids are greater achievers than others, so don't wait for the straight-A report card to do something special. If your child works extra hard to get a B, take him out to lunch and tell him how proud you are.

You don't have to make a big deal out of every single thing your child does, however. It's important for kids to know that a good deed is reward in and of itself and that the world doesn't owe them gratitude every time they do the right thing. If you celebrate more than acts and actions, you help keep life in a healthy perspective.

Throw a party for the first day of spring or the shortest day of the year. Send invitations handmade by your kids. Let them plan the games and decorations. Surround yourselves with people whose presence brings you joy.

Find out how another country celebrates a holiday unique to its culture. Broaden your horizons while you appreciate the customs of a larger world.

Celebrate the gift of life itself. Bring an element of celebration into the everyday. Cut a bouquet of fresh flowers and set them on the dinner table. Eat breakfast by candlelight.

Celebrate the gift of your family. There is no better reason to celebrate than gratitude for the love you have for one another.

Maybe your kids will get in the spirit and throw a party for you, just for being the wonderful parent that you are!

The first miracle performed by Jesus in the Gospel of John is turning water into wine at a wedding at Cana (John 2:1–11). Think about what this story tells us about Jesus. He was at the party, celebrating a joyful occasion, with family and friends. In a very real way, Jesus truly was the life of the party, as he is the life in all the celebrations that honor the joy of life.

Life is a gift, every single day. Celebrate it. When you do, God is there in the midst of it all.

Bible Basic

For where two or three are gathered in my name, I am there among them.

Matthew 18:20

to be continued . . .

If you could throw a party for one person in the world, who would that be, and why?

68 *Make manners matter*

Manners matter. That should go without saying, but sadly, it still needs to be said, over and over again.

Good manners seem to be a lost art. Gone are the days when etiquette books were on the list of reading materials for all young people growing up. Even the word "etiquette" is antiquated.

When it comes to manners, little things count:

- Answer the phone with more than the greeting "Who is this?"
- Say please and thank you.
- Listen without interrupting.
- Say "pardon me?" or "excuse me?" instead of "huh?"
- Chew your food and swallow, then talk. Even the people who love you don't want to see wads of food pulsing around in your mouth.
- Speak in a kind voice to strangers and friends alike. There is no excuse to be rude, even if the waiter brought you a cold cup of coffee. It's surprising how often we speak in the harshest tones of voice to the people we care about the most.
- Thank people with a note or a phone call when you receive a gift.
- Open the door for the other person, regardless of gender or age. Males can open doors for females, females for males, children for adults, adults for children.

Rather than eliminating the need for rules of etiquette, modern technology has made it necessary to add to the list: Silence your cell phone when you're in a meeting, in a movie theater, in church, having a meal. Resist the temptation to send text messages when you're in the middle of a spoken conversation. Talk to your friends face to face, not just on the Internet.

Along with the basics, teach your children a few additional manners that can serve them well as they grow up:

- When you shake hands, use a firm grip. Keep your head up, make eye contact, and smile. Repeat the name of the person you are meeting if it's someone new. "I'm glad to meet you, Mrs. Jones."
- Be on time, especially when someone else's time is involved. Plan to be fifteen minutes early wherever you go. Perpetual tardiness makes it appear as though you think that your time matters more than the other person's. Remember that you are not the only person with a busy schedule. Being punctual is a courtesy to others.

Manners make people feel respected. They make life more pleasant. And they can make a difference when it comes to engaging with a wider world. Which person is more likely to get the job interview, the one who has all the credentials but is rude on the phone or the one who has all the credentials and knows how to be courteous?

Model polite behavior for your child.

Make manners matter. Your child's future husband or wife will thank you!

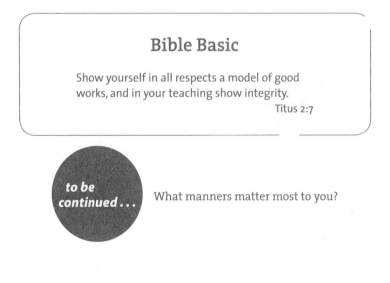

Bible Basic

Show yourself in all respects a model of good works, and in your teaching show integrity.

Titus 2:7

to be continued . . .   What manners matter most to you?

69 *Explore the sacraments*

"Sacrament" is not a word we use in everyday language, except perhaps in church. Teaching children about the sacraments must begin with an understanding of what the word itself means.

A sacrament is a "Christian rite . . . that is believed to have been ordained by Christ and that is held to be a means of divine grace or to be a sign or symbol of a spiritual reality."[26] Sacraments are "signs of the real presence and power of Christ in the Church, symbols of God's action."[27] Baptism and Communion, also known as the Lord's Supper, are recognized as sacraments in all Christian denominations, and some designate additional sacraments (such as confirmation and marriage). Sacraments are visible signs of God's grace that is always active in our lives. Sacraments are recognized through their celebration within the body of faith and lived out through church and family life.

Teaching your child about the meaning of baptism and Communion and living out the understanding of these sacraments in daily life are important responsibilities of Christian parents.

You may choose to have your child baptized as an infant or wait until the child is old enough to understand what the sacrament means. Either way, you need to learn what your denomination teaches about the sacraments. Talk to your minister and find out if the church offers a class for parents and children.

Communion should never be viewed as merely a fun thing to do in church, nor a quick snack. The bread and cup should not be given to a small child just because he's squawking at the fact that other people are "getting bread and juice in church."

Beyond observing and participating in the sacraments during worship, use everyday events to teach your children how these sacraments are part of our ordinary days. When the family is gathered at the dinner table, tell the story of Jesus having supper with his disciples and breaking bread with them (Luke 22:14–20). Share some of the other Bible stories about Jesus having a meal or providing food for others (Matthew

14:13–21, John 6). Ask your children, "Wouldn't it be fun to have Jesus over for dinner? What would we serve, and how would we act?" Then remind them that Jesus is with us when we share a meal together, just as he is with us when we take Communion.

Explore the attributes and uses of water as a way of enriching the meaning of baptism. We can do this when we quench our thirst, splash in the bath, water plants. Our bodies need water to survive. We use water to clean and to grow. What would we do without water?

Ordinary bread and everyday water give us life. Jesus turned these basic elements into a holy way of showing God's love for us. When we participate in the sacraments, and when we think of all life as holy, we make visible the grace of God that we have been given in Jesus Christ.

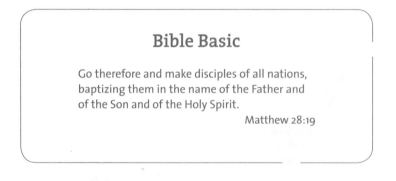

Bible Basic

Go therefore and make disciples of all nations, baptizing them in the name of the Father and of the Son and of the Holy Spirit.

Matthew 28:19

to be
continued . . .

What do the sacraments of baptism and Communion mean to you?

70 *Be the parent*

What is your job as a parent? Making your child happy all the time (which is impossible)? Being your child's best friend? Having your child take care of you?

It is your job to be the parent, and it is your child's job to be a child. You need to be the adult so that your child can be the child.

It's fine to share what's going on in your life, including some of the struggles and difficulties you face with work, friends, health. It helps your child to know that you're grouchy not because of something he did, but because you had a rough day at work or because you aren't feeling well. But don't put your child in the role of the confidante to whom you pour out your woes all the time. Your child will feel the need to solve these problems for you, and that is not a burden that a child should have to bear.

Your child needs to know that you can handle the adult responsibilities. If you're having financial problems, you may have to say, "We are going to have to cut back on the number of times we order pizza, but we can find some great options for pizza at the grocery store, or we can each pick out our favorite topping and make our own." Children can be involved in family dilemmas and problem solving as part of the team effort. However, they should not go to bed at night trying to figure out how to make ends meet or what might happen to the family if you can't pay the rent this month.

Children should not have to worry about taking care of you all the time. Show that you can take care of yourself. It's fine if your child shows a little TLC when you don't feel well or pitches in to help when you work late. Those are valuable contributions to the overall well-being of the family; but the weight of being the mommy, the daddy, the adult of the house should not be on your child's shoulders.

Have confidence in your abilities as a parent. Don't be intimidated by family and friends who question your choices. It's fine to ask for input if you need guidance, but assuming that everyone else has a better answer than you do makes it difficult to make decisions and to follow through. A parent wracked with doubt about his or her abilities leaves a child feeling unsettled and insecure.

Children need to play, to have their own friends, to feel that they are in safe and strong hands when they go to sleep at night. Children need to be children. Adulthood, and all its responsibilities, will come along soon enough.

It's fun to be your child's friend, and that happens when you and your child work together and play together and face life's challenges together. But remember: your goal is not to be a peer, but to be a parent.

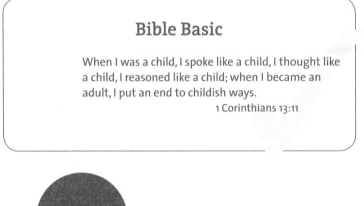

Bible Basic

When I was a child, I spoke like a child, I thought like a child, I reasoned like a child; when I became an adult, I put an end to childish ways.

1 Corinthians 13:11

to be continued . . .

What do you appreciate most about your own parent(s)?

71 *Write letters to your child*

Who doesn't love to get a personal, handwritten letter in the mail?

Letter writing is being replaced by e-mail, text messages, and generic Christmas letters. The joy of receiving a personal card or letter, in a loved one's handwriting, may be a legacy our own children never have.

Keeping an open communication with your children is your responsibility and privilege as a parent. Letter writing is one way to do this.

Children love to get mail, because it makes them feel special, just as you feel special when someone takes the time to write to you.

You don't have to wait until your child leaves home to send a personal letter. Write one now. The occasion for the letter could be a special event, like a birthday or graduation; or it may be no more than your taking an opportunity to put down on paper a few things you say to your child every day, like "I'm so glad to be your Dad!" or "I love you" (you do say that to your child every day, right?).

Place the finished letter under your child's pillow or next to his plate at the dinner table. Part of the fun is for your child to discover something unexpected, something special just for her.

Have an open diary exchange. In a blank book or spiral notebook, write a note to your child on the first page. Leave it where your child can find it when she goes to bed or gets up in the morning.

Now, it's your child's turn to write to you.

Using the same notebook, your child can either respond to what you've written or start a new topic. Words aren't the only way to communicate. Tape a photograph in the diary. Draw a picture. Copy a poem or write your own.

The notebook can be an occasional activity. Try not to get caught up in "whose turn is it?" or "why didn't you answer my letter?" You may each go through spells where you just don't feel like writing or don't have the time. The open journal isn't meant to be an obligation, but rather a joy.

The great thing about letters is not only the thrill you get when you receive one, but the way you can tuck them away and go back and reread them time and time again.

Think of the apostle Paul. There was a guy who liked to write letters! A major portion of the New Testament is made up of letters that Paul wrote to the new churches. We would be missing a lot if we didn't have those letters to guide us in our faith. Paul never imagined that his letters would be read by so large an audience. If he had, he might have asked for an editor before he sent them!

Finding a handwritten letter in that stack of junk mail and bills can make your day. Maybe you can make someone's day by making sure that happens to someone this week.

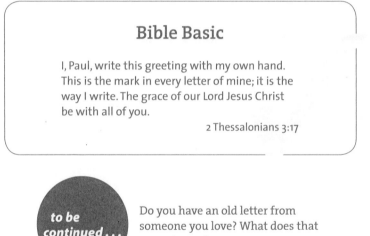

Bible Basic

I, Paul, write this greeting with my own hand. This is the mark in every letter of mine; it is the way I write. The grace of our Lord Jesus Christ be with all of you.

2 Thessalonians 3:17

to be continued . . .

Do you have an old letter from someone you love? What does that mean to you?

72 *Be a peacemaker*

In one of his very first sermons, Jesus said, "Blessed are the peacemakers, for they will be called children of God" (Matthew 5:9). As children of God, we are called to be peacemakers, and that begins at home.

Notice that Jesus called us to be peace*makers*. An action, an intention, is implied here. Blessed are the peacemakers, the ones who are proactive, who work at bringing peace into the world.

Peace is not an absence of conflict, nor a state of perfect and consistent agreement. We are not all going to agree all the time. That would make for a bland and boring world. Differences of opinion keep life interesting.

Peacemakers find ways to disagree and still have respect for the other person. This requires empathy and understanding, a willingness to view a situation from another person's eyes and heart. When a conflict needs to be resolved, peacemakers work to find equitable solutions that allow both sides to move forward with dignity.

How can we expect the world to be at peace when our own families are not peaceful? Fights, arguments, jealousy, and constant competition among siblings make peace an elusive dream. While conflict and tempers are unavoidable when interacting with others, especially family members, parents can model peacemaking and insist it be part of the family dynamic.

Watch the language you use to talk about someone with whom you disagree. When you have a disagreement with your neighbor and you refer to him as a "stupid idiot," that doesn't teach your child about being a peacemaker. Express your disagreement without belittling others. Language is powerful, and the words we use should not be used to demean another person.

Exhibit patience and calm when in a volatile situation. Calm is contagious and goes a long way toward setting the stage for a peaceful resolution. If your own temper is high, step back and take a few deep breaths. Bring in a third party to help mediate a particularly difficult conflict.

When resolving a conflict between your children, or even between you and your child, try a role reversal. Suggest that "you be the mom and I'll be the kid and let's see what happens." Take turns stepping into the other person's shoes and defending the opposing position. It will help you get a different point of view.

Do not allow interruptions. Use nonviolent ways of resolving disagreement and conflict. Do not hold grudges. Learn to let some things go.

Work as a team, figuring out solutions together. Listen to everyone's ideas. Don't give up on one another.

Blessed are the parents who seek to be peacemakers and peacekeepers, for you shall be called wonderful mothers and fathers!

Bible Basic

Peace I leave with you; my peace I give to you. I do not give to you as the world gives. Do not let your hearts be troubled, and do not let them be afraid.

John 14:27

to be continued . . .

Who is the peacemaker in your family?

73 Teach healthy sexuality

Human sexuality encompasses far more than the mechanics of sex.

Sexuality has to do with the whole of ourselves as beings who live within physical bodies. Sexuality is about self-esteem and body image and treating one another with dignity and respect. It's about rejoicing in the fact that we are created in the image of God, and that includes male and female. Teaching your child healthy sexuality means being comfortable with our human bodies. As frustrating and limiting as these bodies may sometimes be, we cannot live apart from them, nor are we meant to.

Healthy sexuality begins with self-esteem. We need to be comfortable with our bodies, imperfect as they are. This isn't as easy as telling your child, "you're beautiful just the way you are," although that's important. Parents have to be aware of the negative ways that media influence self-image. The idea that one has to look like a supermodel or famous athlete to be attractive sets most of us up for failure. Even supermodels don't look the same in life as they do on a magazine page, where photo retouching and camera angles alter reality.

Try not to be negative about your own body around your children. If you tell your child how beautiful she is but moan and groan about the weight you've gained, the value of your comments to your child will be diminished.

Avoid humor that denigrates others or promotes stereotypes, such as jokes about "dumb blondes." Movies, books, advertisements, and clothing that promote sexuality as a means of getting what we want or that show mistreatment of people and relationships should not be tolerated. Commercials promote the idea that men think about only beer, sex, and fast cars; and women are used to sell these. When your child sees these commercials, take a few minutes to talk about how wrong it is to repeat these stereotypes or to use our bodies to sell products. You can't protect your child from all the images being used, but you can speak up against the commercial use of sexuality.

We should avoid gender stereotypes like "you throw like a girl" or "boys don't cry." What do such statements say to your child?

Use the proper terms for body parts. If you make up euphemisms for penis and vagina, it's clear to your child that you are uncomfortable with the human body. Children need to have the proper language to use for describing sex and sexuality.

Our bodies belong to us, nobody else. Trust your child's instincts if another person makes your child uncomfortable. Reinforce that no means no and that nobody has the right to touch your child in any way that makes your child uneasy. It is never acceptable to use verbal, emotional, or physical force to get our way. God opposes oppression and injustice in any form, and that includes our relationships with other people.

Bible Basic

So God created humankind in his image,
    in the image of God he created them;
    male and female he created them.
God blessed them.

Genesis 1:27–28

to be continued . . .

Who is a good role model of healthy sexuality?

74 *Learn to say no*

Along with "mama" and "dada," one of the first words children learn is "no." And once they learn it, they wear it out.

Time to get dressed! *No.* Finish your breakfast. *No.* Can you put those toys away? *No! No no no no no no NO!*

Despite its overuse, "no" is still a necessary word. Parents need to say no in a variety of situations.

Say no to your child. A life lived with only "yes" is unbalanced and unrealistic. If your child doesn't learn how to accept a no answer, how is that going to work out in the world? Children who are never told no become tyrannical, and nobody wants to be around people who don't know how to take a no.

Children learn to set their own boundaries when parents set a few. They learn to speak up for themselves when they learn to receive and accept a no.

When in doubt about whether to say yes or no, remember that it is always easier to change a no to a yes than a yes to a no.

Say no for your child. Even when our kids are good at saying no to us, they sometimes need help saying no to others. Let your child know that if he or she is in an uncomfortable situation and doesn't know how to get out of it without feeling embarrassed, they can "blame" you. "No, I can't host the youth group at my house this week. My parents won't let me do that on a school night. Sorry."

Say no for yourself. Say no to situations that are toxic for you. The neighbor who always gossips and complains wants to drop by your home, unannounced and often. Next time she comes to the door, say, "No, I can't invite you in today. Now is not a good time." You may end up being the topic of gossip when that neighbor drops in on someone else, but you can't control that. Let it go. Give yourself a pat on the back for finally saying no.

Saying no to good things is more difficult. There are things you want to do, but if you take them on, you might stretch yourself too thin. It's all right to say no to the invitation to serve on a committee at church or school, even if it is a good cause in which you have a deep interest. If accepting it means you will lose the one night a week you've set aside for your family or for yourself, say no. Add, "Ask me again in two years, when my youngest starts school (or when my youngest finishes with school)." There will be a time in your life when you can take on some of the things you don't have time for now.

Bible Basic

Keep hold of instruction; do not let go;
guard her, for she is your life.
Proverbs 4:13

to be continued . . .

When have you wished you had said no but didn't have the nerve?

75 *Fill your home with music*

We know a lot about the Old Testament hero David. From his exploits as a young shepherd boy who slew the mighty Goliath to his reign as a powerful and much-loved king, David's life is an open book. But before he became a hero, David was known for his gifts as a musician. His music soothed King Saul when nothing else brought him peace. David is credited with writing the music and words to many of our most beloved psalms.

Music has the power to lift us to the heights of joy as well as to move us to tears. The French poet and dramatist Victor Hugo wrote, "Music expresses that which cannot be said and on which it is impossible to be silent."[28]

Fill your home with music. Lots of it. All kinds of it. Clap to the beat of your toddler banging out a rhythm with a spoon on his dinner plate. Play background music during dinner. Fall asleep at night to the soothing sounds of classical strings.

Listen to a variety of genres. Try something new. If you love classical music, tune in to a little rock just to see how it sounds. You don't have to love every kind of music, but keep an open mind. You might discover that the jazz that made no sense when you were in high school speaks to your spirit in a new way after you've heard it live on a stage or during a service of worship.

Listen to the music your children like, whether it's The Wiggles or Led Zeppelin (and try not to grit your teeth either way).

Music can make the soul sing and give shape to a creative spirit and energy. Encourage children to try out a musical instrument or two. School bands provide an excellent way for kids to try an instrument. If one instrument isn't right, try something else.

Music lessons aren't just for children. Adults can take up an instrument even in their retirement years. Nothing says you have to start young, and not everybody had the chance to learn to play an instrument as a child.

Concerts at parks, recreation centers, and schools offer an opportunity to sample music without spending a lot of money. Whether or not you're musically inclined, you can appreciate and enjoy the musical gifts of others.

Music is a great outlet to release pent-up frustration and emotions. Whaling away on a guitar or keyboard or drums is a healthy way to let it all out.

Strike up your own band! Haul out kettles and cans, or drag your old clarinet out of the closet and see what you can still do. The Bible says to make a joyful noise, not necessarily a perfect one.

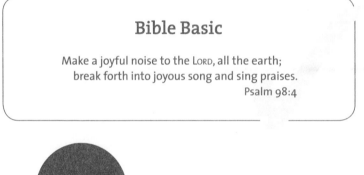

Bible Basic

Make a joyful noise to the Lord, all the earth;
   break forth into joyous song and sing praises.
                                         Psalm 98:4

to be continued . . .   If you could play any instrument, what would it be? Why?

76 *Simplify your life*

Now and then, we all look at the clutter and busyness of our lives and long for a simpler life. We play "Remember when?" Remember when families ate most of their meals together and we didn't rely on fast food? Remember when there weren't five hundred TV channels? Remember when we were kids, before we had jobs and mortgages and children of our own, and life seemed so much simpler?

Now, we have jobs and mortgages and children of our own, and it seems that we can never dig ourselves out from under the stacks of bills and mail and all the papers our kids drag home from church and school. Our calendars are bursting with events and activities and appointments. Without fast food, we'd never eat.

Chances are, our lives are always going to be fairly full of responsibilities, and technology moves ever forward, providing us with more and more ways to invest our time. How will we ever return to a simpler way of life?

The obvious answer is to declutter your life. Get rid of stuff that weighs you down. Resist the temptation to purchase items just because they're on sale. Finish off that bottle of hand lotion before you load up on more. Clean out your closet or one drawer in the kitchen. Don't feel as if you have to answer every e-mail with a long, newsy note.

But there is another answer to this quest for simplicity. Along with seeking to simplify the tangible parts of your life, think about simplicity as an approach to your spiritual life, which is far more important.

Simplicity is a spiritual practice or discipline. Many world religions adhere to simplicity as a way of focusing on our inner, spiritual lives, drawing closer to the divine and the ultimate joy that comes in experiencing a close connection to the source of all life. Simplicity as a spiritual practice requires that we examine our relationship with God and seek to divest ourselves of the barriers that keep us from turning our whole hearts to God.

For example, we get so busy with the stuff of life and all its responsibilities that we put our prayer life on the back burner, where it ceases even to simmer, but grows cold and stale. Why do we neglect this part of our spiritual life that is so crucial and so fulfilling?

Find simple ways to reconnect to God, even—and especially—during a superbusy day.

Offer a breath prayer while you're in line at the grocery store. Take a deep breath in, let it out. Pray silently as you breathe in, "God, you are my God," and as you breathe out, "and I will always praise you." Set the alarm on your cell phone to go off at midday to remind you to say a prayer of thanks. When you're walking the dog, instead of talking on your cell phone, look around and admire God's creation.

Above all, remember that simplifying both your physical and your spiritual life also means being and not just doing. Take a few minutes to sit and rest in God's presence. Don't fill up the space with words and actions. Just be.

Soak in the holiness of knowing that you are loved and cherished by God. It's that simple.

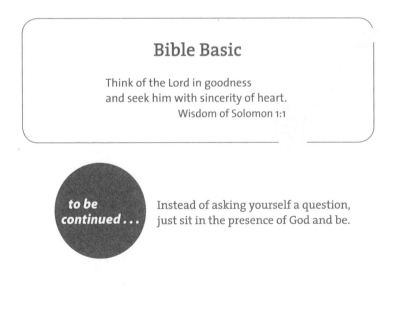

Bible Basic

Think of the Lord in goodness
and seek him with sincerity of heart.
Wisdom of Solomon 1:1

to be continued . . . Instead of asking yourself a question, just sit in the presence of God and be.

77 *Embrace a larger world*

It takes so much time and energy to run our lives. The daily responsibilities of carpools, careers, and keeping up leave us little time to stretch our horizons. The world becomes smaller and smaller, until it becomes defined by the roads we travel to work, school, home, church, the grocery store, and the few square miles in between.

As our own world becomes smaller, so does our focus. Our personal complaints take on a weight out of proportion to their actual worth. If the biggest trauma of the week was that your TV stopped working, it's time to stop and look beyond your own backyard. We gain a clearer perspective when we look outside our boxes and realize that there are billions of other people in the world, many of whom have it a lot tougher than we do.

Though your world may often orbit around your child's needs, children need to know that the whole world doesn't revolve around them. We don't do our children any favors when we make them believe that the world owes them everything. Embrace the larger world, and teach your children to do the same; not because of what they will gain, but because it is the right thing to do.

Have a globe or atlas handy. When there is an earthquake in another part of the world, find out where the country is and pray for the people there. Search the globe for a place that you've never heard of or know little about, and do some research. The names and borders of countries can change as the result of politics and even war. Make revisions on your globe as changes occur.

Volunteer on a regular basis, helping needy people in your own community. In this way, you not only broaden your horizons, you do some good work. Spend one evening each month setting up sleeping mats and packing lunches for a homeless shelter. You and your children will help others and will also appreciate your own home and the gift of having a roof over your heads.

Attend cultural events at museums, parks, and other venues. Experience and celebrate the diversity of the world.

Sponsor a child in another country. The amount your family spends at fast-food restaurants in one week might feed a hungry child elsewhere for several months. Children learn that they can make a difference in another person's life, and this knowledge cultivates compassion and teaches children that they can bring about change for the better.

Learn about the traditions and beliefs of other religions, and mark religious celebrations on your calendars so that you can be aware of the faith practices of people who worship in a different way than you.

God created the whole world, and God loves the whole world, not just our small part of it. The more that we recognize that fact, the more we will be awestruck by the magnitude of God's love.

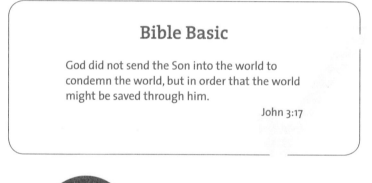

Bible Basic

God did not send the Son into the world to condemn the world, but in order that the world might be saved through him.

John 3:17

to be continued ...

What have you done recently to step outside your own piece of the world?

78 Sprinkle your home with positive thoughts

Along with making sure your family's diet is well balanced, take time each day to plant a few positive thoughts around your home. Positive thinking is an important part of a balanced spiritual diet.

Put books of positive quotations where family members are most likely to pick them up and leaf through the pages. Bathrooms happen to be a good place, but so are kitchens and family rooms, any place your family spends time.

Put the messages from cheerful greeting cards or Bible verses or happy family photos in inexpensive picture frames and place them around your home. Change them from time to time. Keep the family guessing as to what's coming next.

Children can create and decorate the frames and choose items to place in them. Just spending time finding positive thoughts to share develops a positive mind-set.

Pick up a few page-a-day calendars during after-Christmas sales. Place a couple of these where they can't be missed, next to the computer screen, for instance, or in the bathroom. Tear off the pages and tuck them into a lunch box, in dresser and desk drawers, and in the pages of books and magazines. Put them under your child's pillow. Put a few under your own pillow, for that matter. You might need a positive thought to greet you when you finally lay down your head after a long and frustrating day.

Come up with your own ideas about what you can put in the picture frames. Some families post a question of the month that can provide fodder for dinner conversation or a one-on-one chat with your child while you're driving to soccer practice or running an errand.

There's no end to the creative ways you can sprinkle positive thoughts throughout your home. Set your computer screen to run through a list of upbeat images or words. Write your own set of "fortunes" and serve these along with dessert, or place a bowl of them on the kitchen table. Record a happy message for your phone's answering machine, so that your caller gets a cheerful message; and when you're at home and the answering machine picks up before you do, you get to hear a friendly message, perhaps in your child's charming voice. For your cell phone's ring tone, use a song that elicits a smile from you every time you hear it—maybe your family song (see entry 52).

The world can be a negative place, and the news is always full of tragedies and traumas. Counteract the bad news by making your home a place of good news and good cheer.

Bible Basic

A cheerful heart is a good medicine,
    but a downcast spirit dries up the bones.
Proverbs 17:22

to be continued . . .

Can you name ten items of good news that you heard in the past week?

79 *Let anger be expressed*

A young pastor went to visit a couple from her congregation who had been married more than seventy years. "We've never once had an argument or spoken an angry word to each other," the husband said as his wife smiled and nodded. The pastor knew that this couple was the exception rather than the rule. She left her visit with mixed feelings: thoughts of how nice it would be never to have another argument with her own husband, and the recognition that learning how to deal with anger in the context of a loving relationship can be a good thing.

Anger is a valid emotion, as much as joy and sadness and fear, but we are afraid of anger, because we did not learn to express it in a healthy way when we were growing up, or we feel unlovable when we're angry, or we see the frightening effects of displaced and mismanaged anger. But anger can help us identify situations that need to be addressed on a deeper level.

It's what we do with anger—or what we don't do—that is cause for concern. Releasing anger in violent and aggressive ways is not the answer; nor is holding in your anger because you are afraid of it or because it is not accepted in your family. There is a happy balance between these two extremes.

Pay attention to your feelings of anger and discern their origin. When your boss speaks in a demeaning way to your coworker and you get angry, you have a good reason. Let your anger guide you to do something constructive, such as to request a private meeting with your boss where you can express your concern for the way he speaks to those who are under his authority. Anger can point us to a need for action in situations of injustice and cruelty.

When your child expresses anger, acknowledge it and offer constructive ways to release that anger. "Wow, you sure are angry that I made you stay home from school on the day of the Halloween party! It doesn't seem fair, when you have that new costume and have been looking forward to the party for weeks.

But you are sick and need to get better. How about we throw some pillows at the couch and then we'll pile up all those pillows and make a big nest and watch a movie together?"

Physical activity is a great way to release pent-up anger. If need be, buy a punching bag and let your child work out the energy that is elicited by anger in a way that won't hurt another person. Pummeling a punching bag won't turn your child into a violent person. Scream into a paper bag if that helps!

Resolve small issues rather than letting them build up to the point that untangling emotions becomes more difficult. If a particular person continually causes feelings of anger that seem out of proportion to the offense, step back and consider the situation. Why does that person upset you? Regular family meetings and ongoing communication help defuse anger before it spirals out of control.

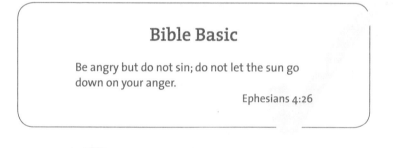

Bible Basic

Be angry but do not sin; do not let the sun go down on your anger.

Ephesians 4:26

to be continued . . .

Are you comfortable expressing and receiving anger?

80 *Stand up for justice*

People of faith are called to do more than take care of themselves and their families. We are also expected to speak up for those whose voices are not heard, those who are victims of oppression and injustice, those who struggle with poverty, homelessness, hunger, and violence. The Old Testament prophet Micah states this responsibility clearly: "What does the LORD require of you but to do justice, and to love kindness, and to walk humbly with your God?" (Micah 6:8). Jesus said that we are to feed the hungry, visit the stranger, clothe the naked, and care for the sick (Matthew 25:34–40) and that when we do these things, we are acting on God's behalf. So it's not a matter of whether we should but how we do, as people of faith, stand up for justice for all of the world's people.

Teach your children at a young age to be aware of the rights and privileges to which all people are entitled. Begin with simple but powerful ways that children can stand up for justice and the rights of all people.

Talk with your child about how to break down walls that keep us from caring about and understanding people who are different from us. What might happen if you sit with the kid in school whom everyone else avoids? Don't go along with the crowd just because it seems like the easy way.

Cheating is never allowed, because it compromises your integrity and makes us feel entitled to something (a good grade, for instance) that doesn't belong to us.

We respect the property of others, be it a sibling's toys or the public park. Don't litter or deface the earth. Pick up the mess your dog makes when you take him for a walk.

Honor handicap parking spaces and restroom stalls, and don't use them unless you qualify to do so. If your church, school, or office building isn't accessible to people with physical limitations, do something about it.

Give generously to organizations that support social and economic justice. Buy fair-trade items whenever possible (if you aren't sure what "fair trade" means, find out at www

.fairtradefederation.org). Encourage your church congregation to sponsor an alternative Christmas market selling fair-trade items and to serve fair-trade coffee and tea at church gatherings.

Support literacy, rain forests, animals, breast cancer research, and other worthy causes. It's as easy as the click of an electronic mouse (www.clicktogive.com).

Express gratitude for the freedoms and rights you have that many in the world do not. Be a responsible voter, and prepare your children to be one as well. Help register people to vote, or work at a polling site, and take your kids along when you vote. Attend town meetings and institute neighborhood watch programs.

We and our children do not need to feel helpless in the face of the world's need when there are so many ways, large and small, to make the world a better place for all people to live.

Bible Basic

What does the Lord require of you
but to do justice, and to love kindness,
and to walk humbly with your God?
Micah 6:8

to be continued . . .

What do you plan to do to stand up for justice?

81 *Express good grief*

Following the unexpected loss of her husband, author Joan Didion wrote, "Grief turns out to be a place none of us know until we reach it."[29] No matter how much we prepare for grief, when it comes we have to plow through it, one painful step at a time.

The work of grief is difficult. Grief takes on many shapes, forms, and lengths, which makes it frightening for people of every age.

Grief is expressed in many ways. A child may withdraw into silence, throw a temper tantrum, cling to his parents. His grades may drop, and he may have trouble getting along with friends. If your child exhibits any of these behaviors, don't panic, but don't ignore them either. They are signs that a child is struggling and needs extra patience and attention.

Give your child opportunities to talk to you or someone else about his feelings or concerns, but don't force it. Timing is important, and everybody has to find their own time as well as their own ways to grieve.

You may prefer to deal with your grief privately or by yourself, but when it comes to your child, don't hesitate to enlist the help of teachers, doctors, counselors, child-care providers, pastors, friends. If you are grieving a loss at the same time as your child, get the help you need and let others support both you and your child. It can be extremely difficult to help your child process her grief when you are overwhelmed by your own. Provide your child with outlets for grief. If she likes to write, encourage her to express her feelings in poetry or journaling. If he finds solace in music, give him ways to express himself through it.

If you are grieving, don't shut yourself off from your children. It's frightening for a child to feel helpless in the face of a parent's sadness. Let your child comfort you. We want to protect our children from our sorrow and tears or from a sad situation, but children are perceptive. It is unsettling for a child to be kept in the dark. Be honest. "Grandpa is very sick. I don't want you to worry, and I promise to let you know how he's doing, because I know that you love him. We'll get through this together."

Don't underestimate the power of your own methods of grieving. How you deal with grief affects how your child deals with grief. It is not a sign of weakness to cry or be sad. Jesus wept over the city of Jerusalem and at the grave of his friend Lazarus. Grief is a natural and appropriate response to a heart-wrenching loss.

If your child is the one grieving, let her know that you believe in her and that she is going to be all right. She is going to get through this, and you will help, as will others.

One of the greatest gifts we can give our children is to have hope in the midst of sorrow and loss. Nothing can separate us from the love of God, and sorrow does not have the last word. We are people of hope, even in the midst of our sorrow.

Bible Basic

But we do not want you to be uninformed, brothers and sisters, about those who have died, so that you may not grieve as others do who have no hope.

1 Thessalonians 4:13

to be continued . . .

What brings you comfort when you are grieving?

82 Write an affirmation of faith

Week after week, worshipers hear the word of God preached by clergy who are trained to study the Scripture and use reliable resources to interpret this word to a congregation.

Thousands upon thousands of books have been written in an attempt to understand and explain the doctrines of faith.

What if someone asked you to sum up in one page what you believe? It would be a challenge well worth taking, because we each should be able to articulate our beliefs in our own words, not the words of preachers and theologians. As you help your children learn to articulate their faith and belief, it makes sense for you to be able to put into words your own affirmation of faith.

Fold a sheet of paper in half horizontally, then in half again vertically. This gives you four squares in which to organize your thoughts. Write "God" in the first square, "Jesus" in the second, "Holy Spirit" in the third, and "Life" in the fourth. The first three categories are somewhat obvious; the fourth, "Life," is to express your beliefs about how the first three connect to all life, and to yours in particular.

Jot down the first words and thoughts that come to your mind for each of the categories. Don't feel as though you have to make comprehensive notes in one try. Let your notes sit for a while. Make notes "as the Spirit moves you."

Next, form your notes and thoughts into sentences. Limit yourself to no more than five sentences for each of the four themes. Setting limits helps you condense and articulate your beliefs succinctly.

Finish by writing a one-page summary of your beliefs.

Write the date on the paper, and put it in a place you'll know where to find it. Your Bible is a good place for safekeeping.

Your statement of faith may never be quite finished. Edit it whenever you wish. You should look over your words from time

Adapted with permission from Kathleen Long Bostrom, *99 Things to Do between Here and Heaven* (Louisville, KY: Westminster John Knox Press, 2009), 90–91.

to time. Faith should be living and real, and expressing your changing understanding of faith and life ought to be a lifelong journey. As you confront new challenges and joys, figure out how your faith informs your response, your understanding, your growth as a Christian in a changing world.

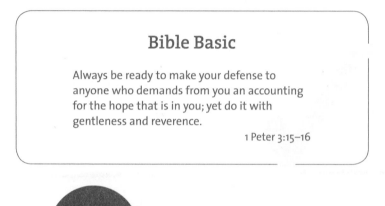

Bible Basic

Always be ready to make your defense to anyone who demands from you an accounting for the hope that is in you; yet do it with gentleness and reverence.

1 Peter 3:15–16

to be continued . . . Can you sum up your faith in one sentence?

8**3** *Give and receive forgiveness*

Your children have gotten into yet another squabble, angry words have been exchanged, and perhaps a little physical tussling added to the mix. In an effort to get past the incident and back on track, you make your kids stand face to face and issue this command: "Say you're sorry and give each other a hug." While your intentions are to bring about peace and reconciliation, the forced words and actions feel insincere, because they are.

A young teen and his mother had a huge argument one morning, and both felt wounded by what each felt to be unfair accusations. The mother, recognizing that she had overreacted to her teen's behavior, apologized. The teen responded, "Even though you say you're sorry, I'm still feeling angry." That's an honest response, and one that should be honored. The mother acknowledged this. "It's OK for you to be angry. You let me know when you're ready to move on." Later that day, the two reconciled, as both knew deep down that they would.

Forgiveness cannot be forced. It must be given and received by a willing heart.

One of the toughest realities about forgiveness is that it isn't always reciprocal. We think that in order for us to forgive, the person who hurt or offended us has to be sorry. We forgive when we believe the other person is truly repentant and has acknowledged his wrongdoing, but that limits the situations where forgiveness can occur. Many times we forgive someone who is not and may never be sorry, because it is the only way we can let go of our hurt and anger and move on. When we hold grudges or hang on to anger and pain, we hurt ourselves more than anyone else. We also make life difficult for our loved ones who may tire of our constant replaying of a grievance and who feel helpless to help us work through our pain.

Forgiving doesn't always mean forgetting. We may forgive the friend who lied about us, but we probably won't forget. We need to acknowledge how deeply the friend has hurt us before we forgive, and then we can move on.

Giving and receiving forgiveness is one of the foundations of the Christian faith. It is included in the Lord's Prayer: "And forgive us our sins, for we ourselves forgive everyone indebted to us" (Luke 11:4). On the cross, Jesus asks God to forgive the people, "for they do not know what they are doing" (Luke 23:34). In Paul's Letter to the Ephesians, he admonishes the new Christians to "be kind to one another, tenderhearted, forgiving one another, as God in Christ has forgiven you" (Ephesians 4:32). We all need forgiveness, and we receive that forgiveness through Christ. Remembering this challenges us to give and receive forgiveness in our daily lives and to live with the joy and freedom that comes to us through Christ.

Forgiveness cannot be forced, neither the giving nor the receiving of it. That's why it is an act of faith to be on either end of the exchange.

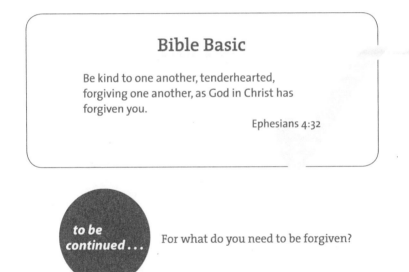

Bible Basic

Be kind to one another, tenderhearted, forgiving one another, as God in Christ has forgiven you.

Ephesians 4:32

to be continued . . .   For what do you need to be forgiven?

84 *Respect privacy*

This book offers many ideas about how to build a healthy family, emphasizing the importance of togetherness. In the midst of sharing living space day in and day out, it is also crucial to respect one another's need for privacy.

Privacy feels like a luxury when children come into our lives. Gone are the days when we took a shower without prying eyes or even had time to think a few private thoughts. Perhaps that's the place to start: permission to protect our own privacy as best as we can, for our sake, and so that our children learn that privacy is something we respect as a family. Unless you really want an audience when you're going to the bathroom, close the door and tell your kids that you expect to be left alone until you're finished.

Parents aren't the only ones who crave a little privacy. Imagine life from a child's point of view, where it often seems as though everything is open to scrutiny. Just as you need some privacy, so does your child.

If your child confides in you, treasure that confidence. You may be tempted to share it with your best friend, if only because you were deeply touched by what your child told you. But think about how you feel when someone you trust breaks a confidence, even if it's unintentional. Ask your child, "Do you mind if I tell Grandma that story? I think she'd enjoy hearing it." If your child agrees, then it's fine; but if she says no, then respect her choice and keep the story between the two of you. Your child will be more likely to keep talking to you if he knows you're not going to repeat everything he says and does.

The world can be noisy and overwhelming and so can the family home. If a child chooses to go in her room and close the door for a while, don't be alarmed. When your child has a friend over and little brother wants to tag along everywhere, protect your older child's right to have some privacy.

Make a point of letting everyone open their own mail. If you have a reason to question a piece of mail that is addressed to your child, ask him about it.

When your child is very young, you sort through dresser drawers to clean out clothes and toys that have been outgrown.

As your child becomes old enough to be responsible for his own things, step back a bit. When it's time to clean out the closet, do this with your child if he needs help. Resist the urge to go through his belongings when he's not around, which is especially tempting as your child gets more involved with the outside world and other people. Parents try to justify this invasion as their way of knowing what the child is thinking and doing. Sometimes you are concerned for a good reason. But once you've violated your child's privacy by reading her diary or snooping through her dresser drawers, you'll be hard-pressed to gain back her trust.

When we respect the privacy of our children, we are doing more than giving them a little personal time. We are teaching responsibility and trust. And if we give privacy, we might receive a little bit, too. Think about that the next time you take a shower!

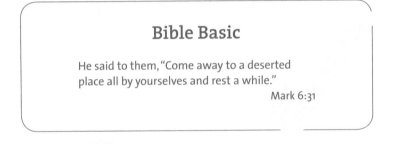

Bible Basic

He said to them, "Come away to a deserted place all by yourselves and rest a while."

Mark 6:31

to be continued . . .

If you had one hour of privacy every day, how would you use it?

85 *Anticipate the good*

Being a parent can feel like a constant process of putting out fires while trying to avoid the ones that haven't yet been ignited. "The baby's sick, and I have a big meeting at work tomorrow. What if I end up sick, too? What if the sitter can't come? What if we get another snowstorm and the car breaks down? What if . . . ?" (Fill in the blank with another possible disaster.)

As we juggle all the pieces that we have to keep in the air, we run the risk of getting caught up in anticipating the next crisis, the next disaster, the next problem. We become negative thinkers, even if all we meant to do was to be prepared for the worst.

This negative thinking extends to the way we approach the everyday risks our children are bound to take: "If you climb that tree, you're going to fall and break a leg! If you try out for the school play, you're just going to be disappointed again. If you don't watch where you're going, you know what will happen (something terrible, of course)."

We can train ourselves to be positive thinkers. Instead of anticipating the bad, start to anticipate the good.

What if . . . the neighbor who has often volunteered to watch the baby will be free tomorrow and willing to come over? What if I have a terrific meeting at work and get that raise I've been expecting? What if the storm fizzles out before it gets to us and the sun starts shining?

What if . . . ? (Fill in the blank with something good.)Train yourself to be a positive thinker. Anticipate the good, even if you have to force yourself to think that way. Imagine the good that can happen in any situation, and point that out. "Before you climb that tree, check out the branches and see which ones are within your reach. Hold on tight and look at the view!"

Yes, sometimes the worst will happen. Sometimes it does help to expect what might go wrong so that you can plan for it (by finding a backup babysitter, for example). But remind yourself that nothing is going to happen that is too big for God to handle. God is here to help us face our challenges.

People of faith are called to be people of hope, to live with the anticipation of what is and can be right with the world. Sure, there will always be the possibility of negative, terrible things happening, but anticipating them all the time won't make them go away. Thinking in negative terms simply darkens the moment.

"If the belief in God is to mean anything to a young child, it must be reassuring."[30] Take that good advice on a daily basis.

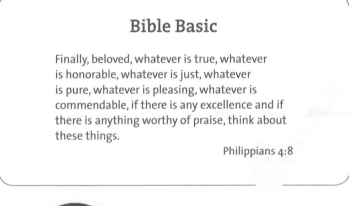

Bible Basic

Finally, beloved, whatever is true, whatever is honorable, whatever is just, whatever is pure, whatever is pleasing, whatever is commendable, if there is any excellence and if there is anything worthy of praise, think about these things.

Philippians 4:8

to be continued . . . What if . . . ? (Fill in the blank with something good.)

86 *Discipline wisely*

The word "discipline" comes from the same root as "disciple," and "discipline" actually means "the instruction given to a disciple." Think of discipline as the ways in which you instruct your child on how to become a responsible and independent person who functions as a healthy member of a family and of society.

"Discipline" and "punishment" are not interchangeable words. Discipline teaches a child how to be responsible for his or her actions; punishment puts the responsibility for the child's behavior on the parent.

You have to figure out how you're going to provide discipline. A good guideline is to "be fair and consistent, but also tender and merciful."[31] Random acts of discipline without logical consequences or consistency create frustration for you and your child and ultimately don't work very well.

As a family, come up with a list of ten family rules everyone must obey. The consequences for breaking the rules should be clear in advance of any infraction, so figure these out together with the rules. "Curfew is 9:00 p.m. on school nights. If you get home past that time, you'll lose an hour next time you're out." Follow through with the consequences, or they will mean nothing. If the rules and consequences are clear and if they are upheld, there is less of a chance of discipline becoming a power struggle between you and your child.

Give yourself moments of peace and calm throughout the day so that you are in a better frame of mind when making decisions about discipline. A five-minute walk around the block before the bus drops off the kids in the afternoon or three minutes of calming music before you begin the after-dinner homework/bedtime/chaos is a good use of your time. Parents get worn down by the tenacity of their children and give in when they shouldn't, which only teaches the children that if they keep pushing, they'll get their way. A tired and frustrated parent is an easy mark for a stubborn and persistent child!

Let children experience the results of their decisions. If a child refuses to eat her lunch, then she goes hungry until the next meal. If he neglects to pick up his toys before school, then he will have to do so when he gets home, thus cutting into his playtime with friends.

When your child misbehaves in public, don't gauge your response by your concern about what others are thinking. Remain consistent with your family's rules. Don't let your child bully you because you're embarrassed by her behavior.

When you lose your temper, address this after you have calmed down. "I am sorry that I yelled at you in front of your friend today. I was tired from work, and the way you were behaving toward your little brother made me angry. Next time, I will ask your friend to leave and then we will work out the problem between you and your brother."

Don't think of discipline as a wearisome and onerous task. Think of it as a way that you help to raise young disciples who are becoming more responsible and independent with each passing day.

Bible Basic

Train children in the right way,
and when old, they will not stray.
Proverbs 22:6

to be continued . . .

How is your philosophy of discipline different from or the same as your parents'?

87 *Be a good listener*

Many people love to talk, but there are very few who know how to listen, who not only make you feel as though they're hanging on to your every word but who actually are. Talking to such a person is a rare and wonderful treat.

You will do your child a great favor if you teach her how to be a good listener. The best way to do this is to be a good listener yourself. You can hone your skills with your child and with adults.

When anyone is talking to you, be attentive. Close the book you're reading, set aside the newspaper, silence the TV, ignore your cell phone. Make eye contact. If you halfheartedly pretend to be listening while you're busy on the Internet, the talker will know and will either feel frustrated or give up trying to talk to you because you don't listen.

If you are in the middle of something that needs to be finished (the book you're reading or the meal you're cooking) and you can't give your full attention, say so. "I want to hear about the report you gave in class today, but right now I have to get dinner on the table. You can tell me all about it while we eat or before we do the dishes. I want to hear every detail!"

Being a good listener doesn't mean you allow yourself to be interrupted when you're talking or when you're doing something else that is also important. A child who constantly interrupts a parent is being rude (as are adults who interrupt). Pause in your conversation and remind the child, "I am talking to Mrs. Jones right now. I'll listen to you when I am finished."

Listening isn't just about being quiet and letting the other person talk, although that's key. A good listener reflects on what the other person is saying and listens carefully to gauge how that person thinks and feels. A good listener doesn't use listening time to figure out what he is going to say next, unless it encourages the dialogue or is relevant to the give-and-take that is part of a conversation.

Practice can help you become a better listener and give you a chance to be heard. Schedule a twenty-minute session with your spouse or another adult. Each person gets ten uninterrupted minutes to share what is on his or her mind (not necessarily thoughts or concerns directly related to the other person). At the end of ten minutes, it's the other person's turn. This is not time for a rebuttal of what the first person said, but an opportunity to talk about thoughts, dreams, concerns, joys. It's a good practice to schedule these "talk and listen" sessions on a regular basis. Parents can get so caught up in the daily routine that spouses get lax about talking to each other the way they did before the kids came along.

Listening is an aspect of prayer that gets neglected far too often. Our prayers become litanies of requests and concerns we spill out to God without taking any time to listen to what God might be trying to say to us. When you pray, allow some quiet time to reflect, concentrate, listen. Taking quiet time for yourself is part of listening to God.

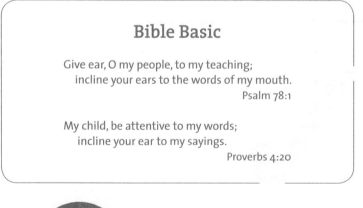

Bible Basic

Give ear, O my people, to my teaching;
  incline your ears to the words of my mouth.
                                        Psalm 78:1

My child, be attentive to my words;
  incline your ear to my sayings.
                                        Proverbs 4:20

to be continued . . .   Who has been a good listener to you?

88 *Be kind to animals*

Children are naturally drawn to animals, so being kind to animals may not seem like a difficult task. Yet caring properly for animals requires more than a loving heart. Learning to properly care for animals teaches children responsibility for the life of another living being and respect for God's commandment to take care of the earth and all its creatures.

No child is too young to learn how to behave with animals. A toddler who cannot resist pulling a dog's tail needs to be taught that this is not only dangerous and hurtful but unacceptable.

Most parents find themselves being begged into getting a pet. Sales of bunny rabbits skyrocket during the Easter season, and dogs, cats, guinea pigs, and hamsters seem like good Christmas presents. Don't bring a pet into your home unless you and your child are both able and willing to give that creature the kind of care and love it deserves. Baby chicks may be adorable when they are tiny, fuzzy, yellow fluff-balls; but what do you plan to do when the cute chick becomes a pecking chicken that poops all over your carpet? Find out what kind of care a pet is going to need. If you can't afford the food and vet bills and if you're not at home enough to give an animal love and attention, then hold off on bringing a pet into your home.

If someone in your home has allergies to pets, your child can still learn to care for God's creatures. Watch birds as a hobby. Set out feeders that attract various birds and learn what kinds of seeds attract the birds that are native to your area. Place birdhouses and birdbaths around your yard or porch. Get some binoculars so that you and your child can observe the birds from a distance. Buy or borrow an illustrated bird book and find out what birds you can expect to find in your area. Keep a journal about the birds you see and their habits. Learn birdcalls, for the fun of it. Join a local bird-watchers' group.

Offer to pet sit in a friend's home. Your child can learn about caring for an animal without the commitment of owning one.

Take a family outing to a zoo or an aquarium. Before you go, or afterward, check out some books from the library. Read poems and stories about animals. Assign each family member a different animal to investigate and then take turns teaching each other about your particular animal.

Learn about endangered animals. Numerous organizations provide information and ways that you can help protect our earth's wildlife.

Being good stewards of God's creation includes picking up water balloon scraps at the park after your child's birthday party, because it is litter but also because birds and animals can choke on those plastic bits. Litter of all kinds is life threatening to fish and wildlife that get tangled in the mess.

Bible Basic

O Lord, how manifold are your works!
In wisdom you have made them all;
the earth is full of your creatures.
Psalm 104:24

to be continued . . .

What was your first pet?

89 *Let your child make decisions about faith*

Your teenager, who has always loved attending church, informs you that he isn't going to attend church services anymore. Your eighth-grader has been in confirmation class all year, but when it comes time to make her affirmation of faith and join the church, she is the only one in the class who opts out, claiming that she isn't even sure she believes in God. Your child is drawn to a religion with doctrine very different from what you hold to be the truth.

Your first reaction may be anger or fear. "Of course, you're still going to church—church is important!" "What do you mean, you don't believe in God? You've always believed in God!" "Surely you don't really believe what those other folks are telling you?" Underlying these reactions is a sense of hurt, shame, or even failure. Why didn't I see this coming? Have all these years I've invested in my child's faith development been in vain? What did I do wrong?

It's hard not to take it personally when your child starts to question the faith in which she has been raised or chooses to express her faith in ways that are different from your own. We want everything to be good for our kids, including a strong faith. If faith is important to us, we're going to want it to be important to our children, so anything that seems like a crack in the faith foundation is going to be unsettling. We want to fix it, make it all OK, but it's not so simple.

This is one of those times when parents need to step back, take a deep breath, and trust. Trust your child to wrestle through the questions. Trust yourself that you haven't failed as a parent. Trust God, that there is a bigger picture, one whose outcome you don't yet know. Trust that your children will come to a clearer and deeper understanding of faith by making decisions and choices that, in the long run, make the faith that they choose and the way they express it real and vital to them.

When our children start to question their faith, it is not a sign of failure. It is a healthy and necessary part of the journey, and the way that our children's faith becomes their faith, not ours, and not anyone else's. That's the way it is supposed to be.

Whether we spend our whole life in a faith environment or come into that later in life, somewhere along the line we each need to claim what we believe and what we don't. We need to examine what we've been taught and decide, "Yes, I do believe all these things," or "That doesn't quite fit for me—so what do I believe?" Everyone needs to ask, "What do I believe about God, and what does that mean for my life? How is God real to me?"

Jesus asked the disciples what people thought about him. Then he asked them, "Apart from what everyone else thinks, who do *you* say that I am?" (cf. Matthew 16:13–17). Jesus knew that all the disciples had to answer this question for themselves, based on their experience of Jesus.

Answering that question is what we are all called to do, too. Give your child the basic tools, and let her build on the foundation that you have begun.

Bible Basic

They are to do good, to be rich in good works, generous, and ready to share, thus storing up for themselves the treasure of a good foundation for the future, so that they may take hold of the life that really is life.

1 Timothy 6:18–19

to be continued . . .

When did you feel as though your faith had become your own?

90 *Make space to breathe*

Schedules and calendars are meant to help us organize our lives so that we can keep track of our activities and responsibilities in a manageable way. What often happens, albeit unintentionally, is that we become bound to these schedules, to the lists of events that fill the hours of every day. Each day is crammed with meetings, activities, things to do, and places to be. We lose what is known as breathing space.

Breathing space is time that is unfettered by dos and don'ts. Breathing space is time when we have no place to be and nothing to do except to be. Breathing space is a rare commodity in most busy families. And breathing space is often where the holy happens.

Just as we are usually much better at telling God what we want than we are at listening to God for the answers and direction we seek, so too we are better at filling space than we are at emptying it. But uncluttered, unplanned breathing space is necessary for the Holy Spirit to stir our spirit with creative energy and with peace. When we are quiet in our souls the "still small voice" (1 Kings 19:12 KJV) of God can be most clearly heard.

Parents need this breathing space, but so do children and families as a whole. If your family time is always busy, busy, busy, then you may have to schedule some breathing space along with everything else that fills the calendar. Block out several chunks of time each week for space to breathe (use the code "S2B" for space 2 breathe). Allot sections at various times of the day—morning, afternoon, evening, weekends—so that you have your personal S2B and so that your family has S2B family time.

Space to breathe gives families restful, laid-back time. During S2B, you'll have opportunities for conversations that otherwise would not take place. Some of the most precious conversations you'll ever have with your child are the ones that aren't planned. And the quiet time is often just as holy. Rocking a child to sleep, snuggling together on the couch reading, watching the sun set with your teenager: you can't put a price on these holy moments. No words need even be spoken.

Space to breathe lets your mealtime be leisurely and unrushed, which is a marvelous and rare gift in a busy family. It provides families with time to play and reenergize instead of cramming in the next obligation, and it allows room for unplanned activities that come up at the last minute.

God works some of the most amazing miracles in us when we allow the Spirit a little S2B within us. It's a good lesson for parents to learn and a good practice to hand down to your children, because someday, they'll be the ones planning family calendars. Wouldn't it be nice to know that they are making S2B a priority? If children are given some space to breathe as they grow, they learn to value it not as a luxury but as a necessary part of spiritual enrichment and spiritual health.

Bible Basic

Now there was a great wind, so strong that it was splitting mountains and breaking rocks in pieces before the Lord, but the Lord was not in the wind; and after the wind an earthquake, but the Lord was not in the earthquake; and after the earthquake a fire, but the Lord was not in the fire; and after the fire a sound of sheer silence.

1 Kings 19:11–12

to be continued . . .

How many hours have you spent this week allowing yourself space to breathe?

91 *Examine your expectations*

We all have dreams about what we want out of life. We imagine the ideal soul mate, envision the children we will someday have, plan and study for a vocation that is fulfilling and lucrative.

Life doesn't always meet our expectations, and when it doesn't, we have a choice: Do we linger in a state of anger, bitterness, or despair, clinging to the thought that life isn't fair and there is nothing we can do to change it? Or do we reconfigure our expectations, set new goals, shift gears, and move forward?

It's fine to have expectations; life becomes aimless when we don't. The secret to living a contented life is to have flexible expectations; to set goals, but not to be destroyed when they aren't achieved. When our expectations exceed reality, it's time to step back a bit and come up with some alternatives.

Ask yourself: What makes you feel full, satisfied, content? Do you covet a larger house because you need the space or because you want more than what you already have, even though what you have is sufficient? Can you decide to be happy with the house you have, even if it isn't your dream house? A bigger house may mean more work: is it worth it to you, or is the time you save in a smaller house worth letting go of your expectations?

Examine your expectations. Know what you *expect* and what you *need*. They're two different things. Needs are what we cannot live without; expectations are guidelines, goals that make us feel satisfied when we achieve them but that we can alter as situations change.

One way to test whether your expectations are unrealistic is to make a list of what makes you happy and what makes you restless. Do you find that you always want more of everything? It could be that something important is lacking in your life. Sometimes our dissatisfaction with life is pointing to a deeper issue that needs to be addressed.

What expectations do you have of yourself as a parent? How do these expectations lead you to do your best, and how do they cause you shame and guilt? You may need to reconfigure the expectations you have of parenting in order to be a better parent.

Examine the expectations you have for your child. Do you demand perfect obedience? Good grades? A clean room? Do you expect your child to be neat and organized when her gifts tend more toward an easygoing, mellow personality? In what ways do you expect your child to be someone he is not? What does this do to your child's self-esteem? You have every right to require certain things of your child, but step back from time to time and examine your expectations. Be sure that they are realistic, and know when to back off.

What are some expectations for your child that help you focus on what's important? Expect your child to be happy. Expect your child to disagree with you. Expect your child to be different from what you always expected a child should be. Expect to be a good parent! Expect the unexpected for a change.

Bible Basic

Let the words of my mouth and the meditation of my heart
be acceptable to you,
O Lord, my rock and my redeemer.

Psalm 19:14

What do you expect of yourself as a parent?

92 *Learn from your child*

Parents are teachers, there's no doubt about it. We may not have the formal education of a professional teacher (although that's not a bad idea!), but we are the primary teachers for our children in all areas of life. Our children learn from us from the moment we first hold them in our arms, and the teaching never ends. They learn from us when we are trying to teach certain skills, and they learn by observing us even when we're not aware of it. We teach by our attitudes as well as by our actions.

Parents are learners, too. Much of what we learn about parenting, we learn the hard way, by trial and error. We learn from what works and what doesn't.

We have plenty of help to guide us in our never-ending role as teachers. There is an endless supply of books on the topic of parenting, from conception and childbirth to the empty nest and beyond. Reading books about parenting is wise, and taking classes on parenting is something any parent should consider seriously. But the very best teachers in the world are right there in your home: your own children. There are no better teachers in the world when it comes to learning about faith and spirituality.

Jesus said, "Let the little children come to me; do not stop them; for it is to such as these that the kingdom of God belongs" (Mark 10:14). When Jesus spoke these words, it was disturbing news to the adults gathered around him, for children were not highly regarded in those days. Even though we live in a child-oriented society, there is a deep truth in Jesus' words for all of us grown-ups, because we, too, must come to God as children.

What does that mean? To come to God as a child is to regain a sense of joy, wonder, curiosity, and trust that comes so naturally to the youngest among us. Children teach us how to know and love God. Learn from your child.

Children have a marvelous sense of wonder. They are curious about everything. The world is a fascinating place, and children are eager to learn it all. Hold an egg in your hand and marvel at how delicate and sturdy it is. Crack it open and appreciate the bright yellow yolk and the way the egg white cradles the yolk. Imagine how life forms inside an egg and then breaks its way into the world. Thank God for the wonder of an egg. Regain the curiosity you've put on the shelf. Learn from your child. It is to such as these that the kingdom of God belongs.

Patience is a virtue we learn from our children, especially because we need to have it in great quantities! Be patient with your child; be patient with yourself. Slow down. Get on your hands and knees and see the world from your child's level, literally. Look at the cracks in the sidewalk, poke around in the ground, smell the scent of the tiniest flower. Learn from your child. It is to such as these that the kingdom of God belongs.

Children ask questions about faith because they want to know and understand God. They haven't yet learned to be cynical; they don't have the roadblocks to faith that we learn as we get older. For children, God is amazing and wonderful and immensely interesting. Peel away your pessimism. Try to trust in God as a child trusts. Learn from your child. It is to such as these that the kingdom of God belongs.

Bible Basic

For it is to such as these that the kingdom of God belongs.

Mark 10:14

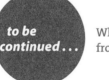
to be continued . . .

What have you learned about God from your child?

93 *Put faith first*

For centuries, people thought that the sun and all the rest of the planets orbited around this world we call home. It wasn't until Copernicus came along in the early 1500s that people discovered that we weren't at the center of the universe.

We may know better now as far as the orbit of the planets is concerned, but we still get confused about what lies at the center of our personal universe. Our lives revolve around all kinds of activities and beliefs: the quest for money, the accumulation of material comforts, the fulfillment of self no matter the cost to our family and friends. These pursuits become our driving force, the focus of our time and efforts; but thinking that they belong at the center of our lives is just as skewed as thinking that the sun revolves around the earth.

Put faith first. Place God at the center of all that you believe, think, and do.

Putting faith first doesn't have to be a dreary and burdensome task. If we begrudge God's proper place, children will pick up on that. If we live faith with a glad and grateful heart, children will pick up on this as well. "Isn't it wonderful that we can pray any time of the day or night and know that God will listen to us?" "We are so fortunate to be able to go to church every Sunday—what better way to start the week?" "Just thinking about how much God loves us brings a smile to my face!"

Adopt this as your family motto: "Faith is not a chore when God is at the core."

We put faith first when we make a priority of the ways in which we express and nurture our faith. We attend church on a regular basis, not just when it's convenient or when we are in crisis. We give our resources, both time and money, even when this stretches us. As with any exercise, stretching is good—it gives us strength. We reach out in service to those who are needy, and we are grateful that we are able to do so.

Put faith first. When you are tempted to take an action that is harmful, unlawful, or contrary to what you believe, then it is helpful to ask yourself, "What would God think about this? How does my faith in God guide the way I live my life?"

Children need to see that faith is not just preached but practiced. In the routine of our daily lives, God is not invisible. Prayer is practiced, the Bible isn't gathering dust on a shelf, and compassion becomes our natural response to the needs we see in the world. Faith is not a chore when God is at the core. Church should be a given in the family schedule, not a dispensable option to be tossed aside when it is inconvenient. You can miss an occasional worship service; that's bound to happen every now and then. But make church a priority, a joyful family time that you and your children anticipate, not dread. Faith is not a chore when God is at the core!

One of the greatest rewards of putting God first is that in doing so, you also put your family at the top of your priorities. Of all the jobs you'll ever have, raising your family is the one at which God most wants you to excel. When you honor your family, you honor God. Faith is not a chore when God is at the core..

Bible Basic

But strive first for the kingdom of God and his righteousness, and all these things will be given to you as well.

Matthew 6:33

 **to be continued . . .**   How did you honor God today?

94 *Remember the big picture*

A new mother told the pediatrician that she was worried that her one-year-old son wasn't eating right. Some days he ate vegetables, some days he refused. Some days he finished everything on his plate—carefully prepared to provide all the major food groups—and some days he refused to eat any vegetable at all. The mom worried that her little boy wouldn't receive proper nutrition if he didn't eat everything at every meal, every day.

The pediatrician, a father of thirteen children, smiled. "Don't worry," he said. "It all balances out over the course of a week or so. Keep providing all the right options, and your son will get the nutrients he needs." Not only were the doctor's words comforting, they gave the mother a model for learning how to balance a lot more than just the basic food groups.

The pediatrician's advice holds true for your child's spiritual nutrition and health, too. Not every day will be a perfect balance, but if you strive to provide the proper nutrients, your child's spiritual diet will be a healthy one.

Some days are better than others. Everything synchronizes with perfect rhythm, and all seems right with the world. Your children sleep through the night (and thus, so do you), and everyone wakes up refreshed. Meals are ready on time, and everyone gathers around the dinner table for pleasant conversation and family devotions. Prayers are prayed before you tuck your child in for the night.

Days like that are few and far between, so cherish them when they come! It may be a while before you get another one.

More likely, we wake up tired and get off to a slow start, which then puts us behind on everything for the rest of the day. The pot roast burns and nobody wants to eat, and the devotional book is lost under the newspaper. All our good intentions go flying out the window. At the end of the day, we feel guilty and discouraged. We meant to do our duty as spiritual leaders of the family, but it just didn't happen.

Don't worry. Remember the big picture. If you strive to put the elements of spiritual nutrition in front of your child on a regular basis, it will balance out as the days go by.

Make prayer a priority—but if you miss a day, don't beat yourself up. If the family devotions don't happen as often as you'd like, don't give up altogether. Rethink the time of day you've set aside for this, and if it isn't working, find another way. If your home is a place where God is welcome and evident, there will be plenty of opportunities for your child to receive spiritual nourishment. Provide the tools of faith for your child, and your child will find a healthy balance in using these tools.

Remember the big picture. This will help when you're having a particularly stressful day and even the slightest inconvenience takes on more weight than it deserves. When a minor problem turns into a huge issue, stop and ask yourself, "Is it really going to matter tomorrow if the beds didn't get made today?" The beds get made more often than not, so missing a time or two isn't the end of the world. Maybe Sunday should be a weekly day off from making beds.

Bible Basic

Why are you cast down, O my soul,
    and why are you disquieted within me?
Hope in God; for I shall again praise him,
    my help and my God.

Psalm 42:5–6

to be continued . . .

What is the best "spiritual nutrition" advice you ever received?

95 *Live a life of stewardship*

"**Stewardship**" **isn't** a term most people use outside of church. The word "stewardship" often brings to mind the church's asking for money during the annual stewardship drive. Just the word "stewardship" makes many people tune out.

But stewardship is not just about money. In the Christian faith, stewardship has more to do with how we see the world than with the amount of money we pledge each year.

Living a life of stewardship begins with seeing everything as first and foremost belonging to God. As Psalm 24:1 says, "The earth is the Lord's and all that is in it, the world, and those who live in it." When we see all the world and all that we have as God's, it changes our view in many ways.

In the beginning of creation, God asked humankind to be stewards, caregivers, of creation. We are stewards of the earth, but in addition to that, we are stewards of the world's people, of our own families, of our worldly goods, and of the faith.

One of the hallmarks of the early church was the way in which the followers of Christ pooled their resources so that they could be generous to those in need. This attitude freed the early Christians from a bondage to material goods and at the same time allowed them to take care of one another, and especially those who had nobody else to look out for them. How would it change your thinking about your possessions (no matter how hard you may have worked to earn them) if you considered them to belong not to you, but to God?

If children see their parents sharing their resources with others, they learn that this is a good and worthy thing to do. Make a day of going through closets and gathering clothing, toys, and household items to give away. Don't just pick your castoffs or buttonless shirts. Do you have a tendency to hoard things you no longer need, or never use, for a rainy day? Consider the folks who are in the midst of a storm right now. When you're shopping for groceries, pick up double an item or two to take to a food pantry or share with a neighbor. When it's your birthday, request a gift that provides for someone in greater need. For instance, Heifer International provides livestock for families around the world whose lives depend on what they can produce from their own resources. A generous spirit on your part will teach far more than mere words can ever do.

Living a life of stewardship dispels our sense of entitlement and brings about a spirit of gratitude instead.

The sense of stewardship extends to how we view the gift of parenthood. Consider that your children ultimately belong to God. As parents, we are blessed to be their caregivers during our time on earth. In addition, we are called to be stewards of each other's children, nurturing, loving, and protecting those to whom the kingdom of God belongs.

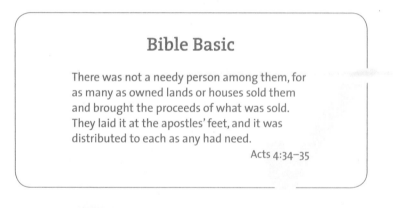

Bible Basic

There was not a needy person among them, for as many as owned lands or houses sold them and brought the proceeds of what was sold. They laid it at the apostles' feet, and it was distributed to each as any had need.

Acts 4:34–35

to be continued . . .

In what ways does your family echo the lifestyle of the early Christians?

96 *Give up guilt*

In the United States of America, in a court of law an individual charged with a crime is presumed innocent until proven guilty. The burden of proof is the responsibility of the prosecution. This law is meant to protect innocent people from being penalized for a crime they did not commit.

In matters of faith, it seems that we take a different approach. The apostle Paul writes in the book of Romans that "all have sinned and fall short of the glory of God" (Romans 3:23). Paul wrote these words to explain to new Christians that every person is in need of God's forgiveness and grace. Nobody is better than anybody else. We are all in the same boat when it comes to depending on God to bail us out. As Frederick Buechner writes, "It is about as hard to absolve yourself of your own guilt as it is to sit in your own lap."[32] We cannot earn God's grace by doing good deeds, but neither are we to live under the burden of guilt.

Guilt is not meant to weigh us down under an unbearable load that causes us to slink through our days, bent over and staring at the ground. Guilt leads us to the recognition that we can't go it alone. We need to hand the load over to God and receive the grace that Christ is aching to give us if we open our clenched fists and hold out our hands. Because of the death and resurrection of Jesus, we "are now justified by his grace as a gift, through the redemption that is in Christ Jesus" (Romans 3:24).

Guilt can point us to an error in judgment, a wrongdoing that needs to be righted. Guilt serves a healthy purpose if it leads us to make a change for the better and to seek God's assistance in doing so.

But if we wallow in our guilt, we miss the point. "Woe is me, I'm such a terrible person, I can't do anything right, and it's all my fault. I deserve everything bad that happens to me." It is tiresome and frustrating to be in the presence of a person who carries such an attitude. It is even more wearying to be that person. Give up the guilt. Give it up to God.

Guilting your child into obedience and good behavior does not promote spiritual health. Children need to learn right from wrong, but bashing them with guilt is not the way to teach this. Guilt without grace gets us nowhere. Correct your child, and have consequences for poor judgment or harmful behavior, but frame this with the promise of forgiveness and renewed opportunities for setting things right. Guilt alone is not enough to guide a child onto the right path. More often than not, the child who feels guilty all the time is going to find ways to hide his wrongdoing and will feel hopeless at ever being good enough.

The joy of the Christian faith is that we aren't supposed to drag our guilt with us wherever we go. Give up the guilt! Give it up to God. Grab the grace of Christ with both hands and with a heart wide open. Believe and live the good news that nothing "will be able to separate us from the love of God in Christ Jesus our Lord" (Romans 8:39).

Bible Basic

Then I acknowledged my sin to you,
    and I did not hide my iniquity;
I said, "I will confess my transgressions to the LORD,"
    and you forgave the guilt of my sin.

Psalm 32:5

to be continued . . .

What guilt do you carry that you need to let go of and give to God?

97 *Memorize Scripture*

It is impressive when someone quotes numerous passages from the Bible by memory. But the number of Bible verses a person is able to memorize may not be a sign of spiritual health so much as a sign of a photographic memory. Seeking to understand what these verses mean and figuring out how you are going to live the truths of the Bible is more important than memorizing the words. Still, memorizing Bible verses is an excellent way to bring the Scripture into your daily life.

Keeping a number of Bible verses tucked away in your heart will provide you and your child a storehouse of good advice and spiritual nourishment to guide you through life's challenges and to give you wisdom when you need it most.

Memorization does not come easily to everyone, so be reasonable with the goals that you and your child set. Choose bite-size pieces of Scripture to begin with—a few words, a sentence or two—it's not the length that matters. Read the verse aloud several times, having fun with the sound of the words, the tone of voice you use.

Practice reading back and forth: you say one line, and your child says the next, and so on. This works well with a psalm that has a repeating refrain, such as Psalm 136:1–3: ". . . for [God's] steadfast love endures forever."

Choose a verse that you repeat with your child every morning and at night before bed. A good verse to start the day is Psalm 118:24: "This is the day that the LORD has made; let us rejoice and be glad in it."

Write the verses on note cards that you can place around the house or tuck into a pocket for reference during the day. Writing reinforces the learning of the words, and your child can practice penmanship at the same time.

Set a Bible verse to music, using a familiar tune.

Make a set of flash cards with Bible verses. Write the verse on one side, and on the other paste a photo or picture from a magazine that serves as a clue. For example, write the words of John 8:12 ("I am the light of the world") on one side and have your child draw a candle or the sun or a lightbulb on the other side. Illustrating Bible verses can also be a fun memorization tool.

When you choose a Bible verse to memorize with your child, ask a few questions: What do the words mean to you? How do they make you feel? What do you think God wants you to remember from this verse?

Think of the memorization of Bible verses as similar to maintaining the proper supplies in a first-aid kit. It's well worth the time and effort to make sure you're always well stocked and prepared.

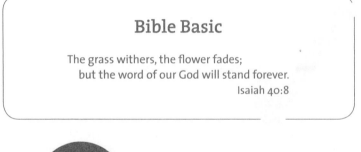

Bible Basic

The grass withers, the flower fades;
but the word of our God will stand forever.
Isaiah 40:8

to be
continued . . .   What is your favorite Bible verse?

98 *Overflow with grace*

Grace is far more than the words we utter before a meal. Grace is the keystone of the Christian faith.

"For by grace you have been saved through faith, and this is not your own doing; it is the gift of God," Paul writes in Ephesians 2:8. We can do nothing to earn grace; it is not our doing, but God's. Even though we do not deserve the loving forgiveness of God, God hands it to us, not on a silver platter, but on the cross and at the door of the empty tomb.

Grace cannot be earned, and God does not force grace upon us. Grace must be received by a willing heart. If we continually open our hearts to the grace of God, and of other people, then we will be able to receive that grace when it is offered to us. A family cannot be spiritually healthy without grace being exchanged by its members. A family without grace is a family where God cannot dwell.

In his book *Never Mind the Joneses*, Tim Stafford writes, "Grace is an attitude and a perspective so basic that it transforms whatever raw material it touches."[33] A family that overflows with grace is a family in which the prevailing attitude toward all of life—and toward each family member— is one of forgiveness and of truly desiring the best for one another. Grace is letting go of a past hurt or bitterness so that you and your loved ones can move forward without that painful baggage. Grace is thinking the best of the other person. Grace is loving your child when he's at his least lovable and knowing that your child loves you in the same way. Grace is joyful, not begrudging; it is generous, not miserly. Grace can transform a rotten experience into an opportunity for healing.

Have faith in God, have faith in your children, and have faith in your family. Do an act of kindness that is totally unwarranted. When it's your daughter's turn to do the dishes and you know she's had a tough day at school, send her off to take a calming bubble bath while you clean up. When your toddler is out of sorts because he missed his nap and you are tempted to shut him up in his room, try hugging him and holding him instead. When you and your spouse start picking on each other, offer an apology: "I'm sorry I'm in such a crabby mood tonight! Let's rewind and start over." When you are too quick to judge or condemn another person, remind yourself that "There but for the grace of God go I."

Be a family that overflows with grace. By living grace, we receive it. When we receive grace, we cannot help but want to give it, especially to those we hold most dear.

When you say grace at the table, begin by recounting an act of grace that you experienced that day, as either the recipient or the donor. Be conscious of the moments of grace that filter through your life.

Don't just say grace. Live it. Let it overflow.

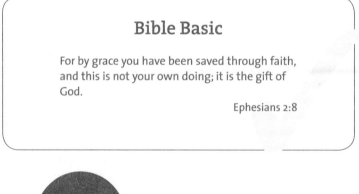

Bible Basic

For by grace you have been saved through faith, and this is not your own doing; it is the gift of God.

Ephesians 2:8

to be continued ...

Where have you shown or received grace this day?

99 *Send your child into the world with joy*

Your ultimate goal as a parent is to let go of your child, to send him into the world with gratitude and joy.

From the moment of your child's birth, she is learning how to be independent of you. This may sound strange, since an infant is so utterly dependent on others for survival and since our instinct as parents is to protect and shelter our children. We teach them honesty, trust, and self-esteem. We make sure their needs for food, clothing, shelter, education, and health are met. We provide them with a loving and safe home; we nurture their faith, skills, and interests. Everything we do as parents is aimed at raising healthy adults who will be able to thrive in the world without us.

There are exceptions, such as children with special needs who cannot live on their own or make adult decisions for themselves. Yet even then, you plan for your child's future without you, because if you both live long enough, that day will come, and you want your child to be capable of survival in a world without you in it.

Claim all that is positive at every stage of your child's development. There are days when we think, "I can't wait until she's potty trained!" or "I don't know if I'll make it through the teen years!" but overall, treasure the moment your child is in right now. Don't wish away the years; they will be gone before you know it. If you continually think about how much better it will be when your child reaches the next milestone, you're going to miss a lot of joy for the place your child is in right now.

Have friends and interests of your own. Your child needs to know that you are going to be OK when he leaves home to attend college in another state or when she moves into her own apartment or gets married. You will miss having your child around, but you are going to be fine. There will be inevitable tears of sadness as your child lets go and moves forward with his life, but along with those tears, be joyful and excited for the new adventures that await your child, and you as well.

Let go of the if onlys: "If only I had been able to stay at home." "If only I hadn't done this or had done that." "If only

I could do it all over again." Let go of the past, and remind yourself of everything you did right along the way.

You'll drive yourself (and your child) crazy if you dwell on all the lasts: The last high school football game. The last graduation. The last summer with a child at home. Instead, rejoice with your child for all the firsts that still lie ahead: The first time traveling with peers. The first time living away from home. The first job out of college. Be happy for all the firsts and not just sad about the lasts.

Rejoice with your child as he heads out the door into the wild, crazy, and wonderful world. As your child embraces adulthood, you will forge a new relationship that wasn't possible when your child was still living under your roof. Pat yourself on the back and say, "Well done, Mom. Good job, Dad. I raised a terrific son, an outstanding daughter. Thank you, God, for giving me the greatest privilege on earth: being a parent."

Bible Basic

For you shall go out in joy,
and be led back in peace
Isaiah 55:12

to be continued . . .

What was the best part for you about going out into the world on your own?

Notes

1. Howard L. Rice, *Reformed Spirituality: An Introduction for Believers* (Louisville, KY: Westminster/John Knox Press, 1991), 45.

2. Elizabeth F. Caldwell, *Leaving Home with Faith* (Cleveland: United Church Press, 2002), 47.

3. Frederick Buechner, *Wishful Thinking: A Seeker's ABC* (San Francisco: HarperSanFrancisco, 1993), 23.

4. William Wordsworth, "Lines Written a Few Miles above Tintern Abbey," *William Wordsworth: Selected Poetry* (Oxford: Oxford University Press, 1994), 58.

5. Sophocles, "Ajax," in *The Tragedies of Sophocles*, trans. Thomas Dale, vol. 1 (London: J. M. Richardson, Cornhill, 1827).

6. Marc Gellman and Thomas Hartman, *How Do You Spell God? Answers to the Big Questions from Around the World* (New York: Morrow Junior Books, 1995), 145–46.

7. Rachel Naomi Remen, *My Grandfather's Blessings: Stories of Strength, Refuge, and Belonging* (New York: Riverhead Books, 2000), 23.

8. Elizabeth F. Caldwell, *Making a Home for Faith* (Cleveland: Pilgrim Press, 2000), vii.

9. Ibid.

10. Elizabeth F. Caldwell, "Religious Instruction: Homemaking," in *Mapping Christian Education: Approaches to Congregational Learning*, ed. Jack Seymour (Nashville: Abingdon, 1997), 88.

11. Robert Wicks, *Crossing the Desert: Learning to Let Go, See Clearly, and Live Simply* (Notre Dame, IN: Sorin Books, 2007), 80.

12. Caldwell, *Making a Home for Faith*, 30.

13. Albert Einstein as quoted in Alan Lightman, *A Sense of the Mysterious* (New York: Vintage Books, 2006), 42.

14. C. Ellis Nelson, *Where Faith Begins* (Louisville, KY: Westminster/John Knox Press, 1967), 10.

15. John H. Westerhoff III, *Bringing Up Children in the Christian Faith* (Minneapolis: Winston Press, 1980), 49.

16. Caldwell, *Making a Home for Faith*, 87.

17. Harold S. Kushner, *When Children Ask about God* (New York: Schocken Books, 1989), 38.

18. Rainer Maria Rilke, *Letters to a Young Poet* (New York: W. W. Norton & Co., 1934), 35.

19. Nanette Sawyer, *Hospitality—The Sacred Art: Discovering the Hidden Spiritual Power of Invitation and Welcome* (Woodstock, VT: Skylight Paths Publishing, 2008), 1.

20. Ibid., 55.

21. Sister Sledge, "We Are Family," *We Are Family*, Cotillon, Atlantic Records, 1979. Use your Internet search engine to fine the lyrics online.

22. Joyce Rupp, *Open the Door: A Journey to the True Self* (Notre Dame, IN: Ave Maria Press, 2008), 130.

23. Vicky Rideout, "Generation M2: Media in the Lives of 8- to 18-Year-Olds," quoted in *Chicago Tribune*, January 20, 2010, Section 1.

24. Elie Wiesel as quoted in Deborah A. Block, "Second Sunday of Advent: Malachi 3:1–4—Pastoral Perspective," *Feasting on the Word: Preaching the Revised Common Lectionary*, Year C, vol. 1 (Louisville, KY: Westminster John Knox Press, 2009), 26.

25. Albert Einstein. BrainyQuote.com, Xplore Inc, 2010. http://www.brainyquote.com/quotes/quotes/a/alberteins165191.html (accessed June 23, 2010).

26. *Merriam-Webster's Online Dictionary*, s.v. "sacrament," http://www.merriam-webster.com/dictionary/sacrament (accessed May 27, 2010).

27. *The Constitution of the Presbyterian Church (U.S.A.)*, Part II, *Book of Order* (Louisville, KY: Office of the General Assembly, Presbyterian Church (U.S.A.), 1999), W-1.3033(2).

28. Wikimedia Foundation contributors, "Victor Hugo," *Wikimedia* Foundation, en.wikiquote.org/wiki/Victor_Hugo (accessed June 23, 2010).

29. Joan Didion, *The Year of Magical Thinking* (New York: Knopf, 2005), 188.

30. Kushner, *When Children Ask about God*, 38.

31. Linda and Richard Eyre, *Teaching Your Children Values* (New York: Simon & Schuster, 1993), 229.

32. Buechner, *Wishful Thinking*, 39.

33. Tim Stafford, *Never Mind the Joneses* (Downers Grove, IL: InterVarsity Press, 2004), 194.

Scripture References

The number in parentheses indicates the number of the entry where this Scripture is quoted.

Old Testament

Genesis 1:27-28 (73)
Genesis 1:31 (44)
Leviticus 27:30-32 (39)
Deuteronomy 5:12-14 (23)
Deuteronomy 6:6-7 (21)
Joshua 24:15 (38)
1 Kings 19:11-12 (90)
2 Chronicles 31:5 (39)
Job 15:3 (41)
Job 36:3 (35)
Psalm 10:1 (2)
Psalm 10:14 (2)
Psalm 19:14 (91)
Psalm 24:1 (95)
Psalm 25:4 (66)
Psalm 28:7a (32)
Psalm 32:5 (96)
Psalm 42:5-6 (94)
Psalm 45:17 (47)
Psalm 46:1 (56)
Psalm 46:10 (59)
Psalm 48:14 (53)
Psalm 51:6 (61)
Psalm 63:5 (58)
Psalm 66:4 (18)
Psalm 68:3 (40)
Psalm 78:1 (87)
Psalm 84:1 (4)
Psalm 96:1 (52)
Psalm 98:4 (75)
Psalm 100:2 (4)

Psalm 104:24 (88)
Psalm 113:3 (50)
Psalm 118:24 (97)
Psalm 119:27 (25)
Psalm 119:105 (63)
Psalm 122:1 (8)
Psalm 131:2 (57)
Psalm 136:1-3 (97)
Psalm 139:7-8 (26)
Proverbs 3:5-6 (1)
Proverbs 4:13 (74)
Proverbs 4:20 (87)
Proverbs 10:22 (13)
Proverbs 15:14 (33)
Proverbs 15:23 (60)
Proverbs 17:22 (78)
Proverbs 20:7 (11)
Proverbs 22:6 (86)
Ecclesiastes 8:15 (9)
Isaiah 18:3 (55)
Isaiah 40:8 (97)
Isaiah 55:12 (99)
Joel 1:3 (54)
Micah 6:8 (80)
Wisdom of Solomon 1:1 (76)

New Testament

Matthew 5:9 (72)
Matthew 5:23-24 (37)
Matthew 6:33 (93)
Matthew 7:12 (3)
Matthew 16:13-17 (89)

Matthew 16:25 (7)
Matthew 18:20 (67)
Matthew 19:14 (22)
Matthew 25:34-40 (80)
Matthew 25:40 (14)
Matthew 28:19 (69)
Mark 6:31 (84)
Mark 9:24 (2)
Mark 10:14 (92)
Luke 1:3 (28)
Luke 11:4 (83)
Luke 17:21 (31)
Luke 22:19 (30)
Luke 23:34 (83)
Luke 24:30-31 (24)
John 3:17 (77)
John 8:12 (97)
John 11:41 (64)
John 14:1-3 (34)
John 14:27 (72)
Acts 4:34-35 (95)
Acts 20:35 (36)
Romans 3:23 (96)
Romans 3:24 (96)
Romans 8:28 (43)
Romans 8:39 (96)
Romans 12:10 (51)
Romans 15:17 (65)
1 Corinthians 3:16, 17b (45)

1 Corinthians 11:12 (27)
1 Corinthians 12:12 (12)
1 Corinthians 12:27 (46)
1 Corinthians 13:11 (70)
2 Corinthians 6:1 (49)
2 Corinthians 8:12-14 (39)
2 Corinthians 9:7 (39)
2 Corinthians 12:9 (29)
Galatians 5:22-23 (62)
Galatians 6:2 (42)
Galatians 6:9 (5)
Galatians 6:10 (16)
Ephesians 2:8 (98)
Ephesians 4:4-6 (17)
Ephesians 4:26 (79)
Ephesians 4:32 (83)
Ephesians 6:19 (20)
Philippians 4:6 (10)
Philippians 4:8 (85)
Colossians 2:6-7 (19)
Colossians 3:12 (3)
1 Thessalonians 4:10-12 (15)
1 Thessalonians 4:13 (81)
2 Thessalonians 3:17 (71)
1 Timothy 6:18-19 (89)
2 Timothy 1:3 (6)
Titus 2:7 (68)
Hebrews 13:2 (48)
1 Peter 3:15-16 (82)